Praise for Susan RoAne and
THE SECRETS OF SAVVY NETWORKING

➤

"Fabulous! A primer on the networking so critical for our professional and personal lives. Susan's 'secrets' are sound and solid... superb tips which will motivate anyone into action."
—Robert Kriegel, Ph.D., author of
If It Ain't Broke... Break It!

➤

"I thought I knew everything about networking until I read *The Secrets of Savvy Networking*. As a sales trainer I recommend every sales manager give this book to every sales person who thinks that there is no business out there!"
—Patricia Fripp, CPAE, past president, The National Speakers Association, author of *Get What You Want*

➤

"*The Secrets of Savvy Networking* is a wonderful 'how-to' book for any individual who wants to understand the ins and outs of making contacts in a positive way."
—William Taylor, CAE, president, American Society of Association Executives

➤

"Surprise! *The Secrets of Savvy Networking* is even better than RoAne's bestselling *How to Work a Room*! This book belongs on EVERYONE'S shelf."
—Dr. Judith Briles, author of *The Confidence Factor and Woman to Woman*

➤

more...

SUSAN ROANE is a professional speaker specializing in keynote presentations to major corporations, professional associations, and universities. She has developed and taught courses in business and management at UCLA, the University of Hawaii, and the University of California at Berkeley. In addition, Ms. RoAne is the creator of such popular seminars as "Nuances of Networking: The Golden Rule Revisited," "Getting Known: In Print...And in Person," and "Building a Base of Business Referrals." She is the author of the best-selling *How to Work a Room*. Ms. RoAne has appeared on many national and local television shows. She lives in San Francisco.

THE SECRETS OF SAVVY NETWORKING

HOW TO MAKE
THE BEST CONNECTIONS— FOR BUSINESS AND PERSONAL SUCCESS

SUSAN ROANE

WARNER BOOKS

A Time Warner Company

Copyright © 1993 by Susan RoAne
All rights reserved.

Warner Books, Inc., 1271 Avenue of the Americas, New York, NY 10020

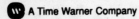 A Time Warner Company

Printed in the United States of America

First Printing: April 1993

10 9 8 7 6 5 4 3 2 1

Library of Congress Cataloging-in-Publication Data

RoAne, Susan
    The secrets of savvy networking / Susan RoAne.
      p.   cm.
    Includes bibliographical references and index.
    ISBN 0-446-39410-6
    1. Social networks—United States—Handbooks, manuals, etc. 2. Business etiquette—United States—Handbooks, manuals, etc. 3. Public relations—United States—Handbooks, manuals, etc. I. Title.
HM131.R6   1993
302.4—dc20   92–31662
                                        CIP

Cover design by Dorothy Wachtenheim
Cover illustration by Mark Fisher
Book design by H. Roberts

Dedicated in memory of

Sally Livingston, my "femtor," who made me aware of the term "networking," taught me the formal process, and confirmed that I had always *lived* it.

Ida (Bobi) Cohen, my grandmother, who sits on my shoulder, whispers in my ear, and inspires me.

▶ ▶ ▶ ▶ ▶ ▶ ▶ ▶ ▶ ▶ ▶ ▶ ▶ ▶ ▶ ▶

CONTENTS

PREFACE

Once in a while we do have to listen to what other people tell us. Especially when that other person is Joann Davis, executive editor at Warner, who acquired *How to Work a Room* for paperback publication. It did take me a couple of conversations to pay attention to Joann's concept for this book. And then my friend Carl LaMell convinced me that she was right. Joann motivated me to go back to my roots and take a look at what I had published over the last twelve years, as well as look at what I do to run my business and how I live my life.

In the pages that follow, I have shared what all of us can do to establish the rapport, communication, and a foundation for relationships and friendships that impact our careers and enrich our lives. In *How to Work a Room*, I taught readers how to mingle, meet new people, start conversations, and make business contacts. Now I am going to amplify on that message. Whether you are a career cop or corporate executive, artist or architect, manager or mechanic, nurse or nun, undertaker or underwriter, banker or broker, realtor or rabbi, firefighter or free-lancer, journalist or job seeker, professor or politician, telemarketer or teacher, I wrote this book for you.

I will provide a blueprint for increasing people skills and expanding your resources. Most of this is not new and none of it is difficult to do. I've just framed it in a simple, accessible way that makes sense. At times, I'll sound like my grandmother... at times, like yours. But they taught us that which will serve us well in the 1990s and the twenty-first century.

This book is for the person who likes and respects people, the person of substance who wants to be a resource and to contribute to others, and the one who appreciates those who have been a resource and contributed to his or her life.

This book promotes a lifestyle of linkages from you to other people whom you know and the people they know: the extended network. This safety net is sturdy and as tightly woven as those used by firefighters in rescue operations. Our networks are crucial in business as well as life. They often come to the rescue!

There are two core issues that I simultaneously espouse: (1) being politically savvy and (2) being respectful, sincere, and considerate. In the chapters that follow, I'm going to teach you to identify the people who can assist you in reaching your goals and show you how to respect their help and nurture it for mutual gains.

Writing a book is a formidable task, but I had fun when I wrote in a light-hearted manner. There is both homework and food for thought here. There are asides, double entendres, and wordplays which made me smile; I hope you will, too.

Susan RoAne

San Francisco, April 1992

ACKNOWLEDGEMENTS

Writing is a solitary process, but I was never alone. My friends, my cronies and my networks were with me. They provided space so that I could become "Esther Sequester" or "Solitary Susan," as my friend Ruthe Hirsch nicknamed me. My friends gave me support, encouragement, empathy, ideas, food for thought, and laughter. They shared their collective experiences, much of which you will read about in this book.

Thank you to those who took the time to fill out our surveys and allowed me to interview them. And to those who provided material that transgressed the boundaries of good taste and good manners, thank you too! We know who you are, even if you don't.

To those who are ever-present, thank you.

To Mumsy (Joyce Siegel), who has always listened, guided, encouraged, and shared insights, reminded me of the task at hand, and gave me a gentle nudge when I wasn't writing.

To Lana Teplick, whose "Oh, *wow*" punctuated her praise for the successful completion of each chapter of this book, and of my life for over twenty-six years.

To Lois Vieira for constant devotion, support, thoughts, and energy, and a great giggle.

To Carl LaMell for mentoring, savvy business sense, great wit and wisdom, and for a unique perspective on all of my problems... for over thirty years.

To my fabulous friends, the network that nurtures me: Sylvia Cherezian for laughter and love, and Ruthe Hirsch, Jean Miller, Judith Briles, Jenni Klein, Teri Skov, Patricia Fripp, Donna Schwarz, Barry Wishner, Sandi Murphy for cartoons, Lisa Miller, Donna Epstein, Griggs RoAne, Dr. Geraldine Alpert, Linda Mantel, Sherris Goodwin, Jim Cathcart, Duke DuBois of GRP Records for marvelous music, and Dave Sikora for his collection of quotes. To Laura Talmus, Ace Smith, and Sandy Lipkowitz for making sure I did not PASS-over the holidays.

To Kerry Davis, who translated the hieroglyphics of my handwriting without a Rosetta Stone.

To Becky Gordon for running the speaking business when I was sequestered and for editing this book. The cartoons you will see had to pass the Gordon Giggle Test.

To my editor, Joann Davis.

To my agent, Sandra Dijkstra.

For this book, there has been a change in the reward system: from M&M's (saving the red ones for last) to S&M of the aerobics classes. To my instructors, who helped me prevent the results of sitting for days from becoming permanent.

Thank you all.

INTRODUCTION

"It's not what you know, but who you know" is a well-known saying. Yet, it is only half-true. The reality is that, in order to manage a career, grow a business or guide your personal or professional endeavors, IT IS WHO KNOWS YOU!

Talent alone will not prevail, nor will skill, experience nor membership in Mensa. It is the contacts you have made, and the connections you have established, that contribute to your success.

What is success? I cannot define it for you. You know what you want, what you value, and what you're willing to do to get "it." "Paying dues" is unavoidable, but you can "negotiate" the payments if you have visibility and viability in your profession, industry, company, and community.

After You Work a Room

Your pockets are bulging with business cards (other people's) because you have just spent three hours, or days, at a meeting or conference. Your arm muscles are sore from shaking hands and your vocal cords are a bit scratchy from shouting over the brass band at the reception. And you are exhausted! You've read *How to Work a Room,* and your ability to "work" a room, and to meet and mingle with strangers, has improved (excelled). Mazel Tov!*

You have worked the room with charm, chutzpah* and gracious manners. All you want to do is soak your aching feet in hot water. But you actually connected with several people whom you would like to meet for coffee, lunch, racquetball. You would like to do business with them! You return to the office, place the cards on your desk, and, *voilà,* the phone rings! An urgent call from a client, colleague, patient, or offspring. More paper is piled on your desk, the cards are "lost," as are the ideas, conversation, and contacts.

"Work smart, not hard" at best tells half the story. Networking is the way to work smart, and you still have to work *hard*! This book will tell you how to do just that. It provides the game plan, rules, and rituals: the *secrets* of savvy networking. Determine your direction, examine your purpose, and parlay your position to benefit your career, company, and community by making a difference.

Some people suffer from the "Walden Pond" problem: individualists who bought the "bootstrap B.S." Making it on your own may work in the wilderness, but not in the job jungle. Interdependence is the law of nature and survival. In the 1990s and the year 2000, we are inextricably intertwined with our colleagues, cronies, and competitors.

According to Marilyn Ferguson in *The Aquarian Conspiracy,*[1] we are benefiting from the phenomenon predicted by Marshall McLuhan: the implosion of information. Global communications have created instantaneous links of networks of people who are poised for communication.

The best definition of networking is the one I learned from my friend the late Sally Livingston. Networking is a "*reciprocal* process based on the *exchange* of ideas, advice, information, referrals, leads, and contacts where resources are *shared* and *acknowledged*." Networking enhances both

*See Glossary.

personal and professional aspects of one's life and increases your power, position and influence, and quality of life.

Information is power only when it is exchanged. Knowing something or someone who is potent and pivotal and keeping it to yourself because of potential harm makes sense. But if there is no risk of harm, information or a contact not shared is worthless on the "Take Stock Exchange."

Corporate America knows it has a problem: It needs networking know-how. In the 1980s the buzzword "networking" was prevalent among women's professional organizations. Individuals realized that developing a personal resource base enhanced their professional lives. Now, in the 1990s, Corporate America needs to learn what Entrepreneurial America knows: how to communicate and connect with networks of people, both professionally and personally.

The recession of 1991–92 increased layoffs in the white-collar arena. Courses, outplacement companies, and job support groups have proliferated, all emphasizing the strategies of networking. No one will be "too busy" to network in the remainder of the nineties and into the next century because it's a preventative measure!

In this book, you will learn how to develop and expand your business base of referrals, the unwritten rules and etiquette of creating a firm foundation, the do's and don'ts of networking, and how to communicate with contacts to create solid business relationships and friendships. And to enjoy the process.

As in *How to Work a Room,* I will smash some myths, share some strategies, and provide examples and illustrations that support my premise: people who are in touch are "in touch."

1

▶ ▶ ▶ ▶ ▶ ▶ ▶ ▶ ▶ ▶ ▶ ▶ ▶ ▶ ▶ ▶ ▶

An Ancient Way to Get Ahead

"No room at the inn! Could you recommend a barn, perhaps, with a manger?"

Does that story sound familiar?

As far back as biblical times, people have relied on whom they know for information or referrals. That is the way we find summer camps for our children, auto mechanics, dentists, good restaurants, and countless other goods and services in our lives. The Yellow Pages are a wonderful resource, but would you use them to identify a cardiologist?[2]

Networking for word-of-mouth advice and personal referrals is a timesaving and an "aggravation management" technique to get recommendations for what we need. We have been exchanging those recommendations and "sharing resources" since Eve offered Adam an apple in the Garden of Eden. It is how the world works—and has, since the beginning of time.

Network: a Verb?

Although English teachers lament the use of nouns as verbs, the word "network" (noun) became an action verb in the early eighties...with emphasis on *action!* Networking is defined by *Webster's Unabridged Encyclopedia Dictionary* as "the act or process of informally sharing information or support, especially among members of a professional group."[3] I'd like to add to that definition.

Networking is a reciprocal process, an *exchange* of ideas, leads, and suggestions that support both our professional and our personal lives. There is also a spirit of sharing that transcends the information shared. The best networkers reflect that spirit with a genuine joy in their "giving."

Networking works for those who appreciate the path and process as well as the destination. I cannot stress enough just how important it is to develop and finely hone your follow-up skills. There is no process of networking, no sharing of information, resource nor referral that occurs without it. Follow-up is not only the focus of this book, it is a basic tenet of life. Behaviors and actions support words; the lack of either subverts them.

Networking in a Nutshell

"The closest thing to knowing something is to know where to find it." Sounds like a brilliant quote from a business strategist or philosopher, or both. Wrong! It was the prevailing problem-solving principle of Mrs. Kurtz, my fifth-grade teacher at Delano Elementary School on Chicago's West Side. She instilled and enforced it as she taught us the Dewey decimal system. We didn't have to be walking encyclopedias; but we did have to be able to think, assess, plan—and walk over to the encyclopedia to find what we needed.

And that is networking in a nutshell! People who have resources are resourceful. People who are willing to open their Rolodex™, pick up a phone, call on their contacts, and ask for help, ideas, and solutions, and who offer leads, information, and ideas, are perceived as powerful and smart. The closest thing to knowing something is to know where and *how* to find it.

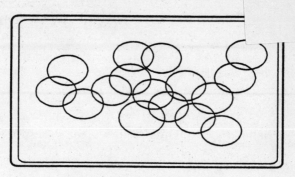

Networks are overlapping circles.
The exchange is in the 20% area of overlap.

Powerful people have linkages that are plentiful, diverse, and expansive—and are able to get things done because of those linkages.

How the Communications Net Works

Although powerful people may be "courted" because they have "pull," everyone has something to contribute, some area that they know well. The trick is finding out what that "something" is. I promise you that if you find out what people *like,* they will know a lot about it and will be willing to share it if you treat them with respect and admiration for their knowledge, skills, and accomplishments. My experience as an educator who spent thirteen years in some volatile classroom situations taught me a valuable lesson. Children live up, or down, to our expectations of them. We all do. If I ever walked into a classroom and said, "You kids are terrible!" Guess what? They were! Let us think highly of the people we meet as we "work rooms" of all types. Let's figure out what makes them special. By conveying positive feedback, we will contribute to people's self-confidence, which encourages the exchange of ideas, information, and support.

Capturing Confidence

I want to inject a word here about self-confidence. We meet people at meetings, parties, conventions, or in the bleachers, at a 10K race, in the balcony of the opera or steam room of the health club. Often they seem so comfortable, conversational, and interesting that by comparison we think we are not. I have a friend who was raised with a great wealth of experiences, people, fascinating stories, and money. He led an exciting, interesting, worldwide, and whirlwind life compared to my upbringing, education, and teaching experience in Chicago and San Francisco. While he was featured in papers, I was grading them! And I must confess that for quite a while I let my impressions of him detract from my self-image. By contrast to my friend, I wondered if I had anything to "bring to the banquet."

I found it helpful to read *The Confidence Factor,* by Judith Briles, who compiled ten commandments of confidence.[4] *Assess the Situation* is Briles's fifth commandment. When we take time to assess who we are, what we have done, and what we know, we will have an *accurate* picture of ourselves. It serves those who feel uncomfortable with their ability to contribute due to lack of confidence, as well as those who possess an inflated self-perception (and who probably have a pumped-up résumé to match).

In the early 1980s Senator Dianne Feinstein, then mayor of San Francisco, spoke at a luncheon hosted by six women's business and professional networks. Feinstein is an eloquent speaker and had prepared a "Ten-Point Plan for Women to Succeed." I will always remember her first recommendation: Become an expert in a particular area. Choose an area of keen interest to you so that you will enjoy the books to be read, conversations to occur, research to be completed, and the diligence required to master the subject.

Feinstein's advice mirrored what I had learned through the National Speakers Association: Become an expert because companies and associations hire experts to speak, to share their expertise. You may possess that body of knowledge right now or may have the foundation upon which you can build. I am, as one organization for which I spoke billed me, the

Mingling Maven.* If you have an area of expertise, you are going to be viewed as a resource by others who may some-day tap your know-how.

What Do You Do? What Do You Know? What Do You Like?

Have you
overlap wi.

Maybe your own interests

Your Personal Interests

HOBBIES
- Avid reader
- Wine connoisseur
- Gourmet cook
- Green thumb

SPORTS
- Sailor
- Runner
- Bungee jumper
- Wind surfer
- Baseball fanatic

WORK
- Financial analyst
- Computer genius
- Team leader
- Composer
- Presenter
- Mechanic
- Keyboards

CULTURAL EXPERIENCES
- Opera buff
- Symphony supporter
- Ballet sponsor
- Theatergoer

AVOCATION
- Glassblowing
- Ornithology
- Stand-up comedy (I know a doctor who does stand-up)
- Jazz piano

COMMUNITY INVOLVEMENT
- Girl Scout leader
- Local theater company board
- Little League coach
- Heart Association

*See Glossary.

There are those days that you are managing a family, career, volunteer commitments, carpools, and homework and still remain sane. That is truly an accomplishment!

The time to assess is now. It is another way of looking in the mirror and helping ourselves gain the confidence we need. It is especially true for women, as we were taught to "defer to the accomplishments of the less accomplished." We can break the mold and move forward.

One way to learn about yourself is by paying attention to compliments.

One of the things I've been told is that I am an empathic listener who listens with my heart. My long-time friend Diane Bennett, a fellow teacher, called to tell me about something wonderful that had happened to her. I was overjoyed for her and said, "Diane, I wish we were together so you could see how happy I am for you." "Susan, it's okay, I can *hear* you feel my joy," she said. *So pay attention to complimentary comments. Write them down so you will remember them. Reread your notes from time to time. You can learn things about yourself that will be affirming, make you feel good, and boost your confidence.*

The Diagramming "Sentence"

While I cannot offer advice on skiing, horseback riding, car maintenance or recipes (no one *ever* asks for mine), I can share ideas with my network about the speaking business, publishing tips, and writing (which was made possible by two years of suffering through seventh- and eighth-grade diagramming of sentences). I am not computer literate (I wrote this book with pencils), but I know how to program my VCR. I even taught a friend how to program hers! Not bad for a total technophobe!

One area I know firsthand is menopause; I have taken a course on the subject, formed a support group, read the literature, and am committed to sharing my knowledge. I have stood on stages before male audiences, with a microphone in one hand

and a fan in the other, having inconvenient hot flashes! (Has there ever been a convenient one?) Simply making it to this point in life has given me a *cause célèbre!* More important, I have learned a great deal from the other knowledgeable women in my group that impacts my health and well-being. So I "warmly" share that knowledge, awareness, and information I have learned from my menopause mavens, "The Red Hot Mamas."™

A friend of mine who has had a family history of heart disease and weight problems is a compendium of facts concerning calories, cholesterol, and grams of fat for every food served. She's a successful financial consultant who truly knows how to trim the fat out of the budget and body and happily shares her knowledge of both...when asked.

Maybe you have a green thumb, coaching skills, financial savvy, computer magic (my perception of those who are technically adept), or are a person of great humor with an infectious laugh. Or perhaps you are a voracious reader, willing to recommend books.

Evangeline Ysmael, free-lance journalist, the former editor of *Speakout,* the newsletter for the National Speakers Association, and an avid mystery reader, knew I had recently returned from Israel and asked if I had heard of Jonathan Kellerman. "He is an excellent writer," she said, "and I am sending you his book. It's set in Jerusalem and you'll get many more of the references and terms than I." Evangeline's enthusiastic recommendation spurred me to read *The Butcher's Theater,* my first mystery. I have since read most of Kellerman's books, as well as those of his wife, Faye Kellerman. My point: Evangeline Ysmael was a valuable resource to me.

Each one of us can make many types of contributions to our networks. The confidence to do so starts with self-assessment. Think for a minute. When was the last time you were asked to recommend a good restaurant, dentist, tailor, mortgage broker, cleaner, florist? Perhaps as recently as today. Remember: Being asked for a recommendation or referral also implies that your opinions are respected. Don't underestimate your potential to contribute something others may find valuable.

Those who do it best often don't know they are networking;

they are just being themselves, willingly sharing resources, ideas, and information.

The Brainstorm Bonus

There is another aspect to the process of networking that is even more valuable: the impromptu brainstorming session—the blending of brainpower to solve problems. Some of us do this in informal settings, while others participate in brain-trust groups. Formal think tanks have been around for years (Hoover Institute at Stanford University is one). Their purpose is to analyze and solve political, social, and economic problems, both domestic and international. "Brainstorming is one of the best aspects of our Business Alliance networking groups. One time I had a problem with a client, and the group's advice saved the client and increased my revenues," shared Irv Spivak of IME Telecom Corp.

Brainstorming is a bonus that occurs in many business settings: conferences, roundtable discussions, hospitality suites, and task force meetings. If we believe that two heads are better than one, then ten heads put you way "ahead" of the ball game, which is also one of the places brainstorming can occur.

Brainstorming sessions take place where groups of people are gathered. You have probably taken part in an informal session with friends, family, neighbors, and colleagues over dinner, at a picnic, in the health club, or before a baseball game. Good networkers are great brainstormers who enjoy sharing ideas and offering solutions. The synergy of minds feeding off one another is exhilarating.

"We do brainstorm for our businesses, careers, and personal lives as a matter of course. It behooves us to take the full networking process seriously and to commit to the required follow-through," according to Eileen McDargh, author of *How to Work for a Living and Still Be Free to Live*. Additionally, she says, because our lives are multifaceted, "we need to surround ourselves with people who support the 'work' of our lives and not just our 'jobs,' which are only where we get our paychecks."

Millionaires Do It

What is the one trait all millionaires have in common? (Hint: It is not $1,000,000.) "A huge Rolodex™," according to Tom Stanley, author of *Marketing to the Affluent.* Even more important than the Rolodex™ is "their networking ability which may be the key to their success."[5] The millionaires knew who were in their card files and were not just willing but also *eager* to share these resources with the other millionaires in their Stanley research groups.

We former English teachers will have to adjust: "Network" is now a verb of action…tremendous action. Yet it is also a verb of sense: common sense!

Getting Higher with a Little Help from Our Friends

"Networking is based on a deeper philosophy than most people realize," according to Barry Wishner, who interviewed 280 CEOs for his forthcoming book, *Get Better or Get Beat.* "Those CEOs were committed to establishing a foundation for win-win relationships. Each one had fascinating stories about their evolution to the top, and most credited the contributions of their networks to their career success."

According to author Michael Korda, "A network is not something you can establish overnight; it's the result of working on it for decades. If you haven't established a network of friends by the time you're forty, you're in trouble."[6]

President Bill Clinton exemplifies the best of networkers. The FOBs (Friends of Bill) were highly visible and very instrumental in his successful presidential campaign. They included friends from his days as a Rhodes scholar, at Yale Law School, and as a Georgetown undergraduate, and some were from his youth in Hot Springs. I learned of their devotion to him when I was a speaker for Arkansas's conference on tourism in Hot Springs several years ago.

Because our lives change, it's practical that we call upon each other for advice, information, ideas, and contacts, whether it's in the classroom, conference room, workstation or lab.

"If there is no communication among colleagues because they lack internal technical networks, parts of research projects may be needlessly and wastefully duplicated," shared Dr. David Sikora, of Monsanto Company's Chemical Group, who enthusiastically supports personal communications networks.

The abilities to communicate and to network contribute to the bottom line. According to Bert Decker, author of *You've Got to Be Believed to Be Heard,* and founder of the Decker method of public speaking, "communication is a contact sport."

Minding Our Manners

While the large Rolodex™ and ability to use it effectively are important to our business, there's another facet of networking that goes beyond the actual linking of resources. It is the "style," or better yet, the manner(s), of matchmaking.

As old-fashioned and Pollyanna-like as it seems, good manners and common courtesy are two very important aspects of the networking process. Unfortunately, they are most noticeable by their absence. When we are training new employees in our office—or even our offspring—to successfully do their jobs, lessons on manners are critical.

We have all had experiences—"war stories"—of dealing with people whose behavior indicates they were raised by wild wolves in the forest, Greystoke notwithstanding (lack of acknowledgement, follow-up, and follow-through). There is a code of behavior in networking, and in business in general, that must be observed. If not, both the name of the individual and his/her company or association may be maligned by the people who have experienced that individual's demeanor.

So let's recap the benefits of networking:
1. We all win when we are open to a process that links people and resources.

2. Our access to information increases by the number of people we know.
3. Working is enhanced by networking in every walk of life.

It reminds me of the old shampoo commercial: "And I told two people, and they told two people," and so on, until the screen was a collage of an exponentially expanded group of women with beautiful, clean hair.

The abilities to communicate, share resources, and network allow us to embrace life and its changes, not just to manage them. Before embarking upon this path, assess the benefits of networking. A potential benefit is that information is power and it give us something to trade. There is formal information that we obtain through memos, company reports, and research. Then there is the all-important informal information that we hear through the grapevine.

The Pros and Cons of Networking

Get a ledger sheet. Fill it in. It will help you make an informed choice about getting involved in the process of networking.

The Ledger Sample

DEBITS	CREDITS
1. Time	1. Ideas
2. Energy	2. Leads
3. Inconvenience	3. Advice
4. $$ Cost	4. Support
5. Obligation	5. Brainstorming
6. Involvement	6. Involvement

"Networking—you've got to *work* at it," advised Kevin Sullivan, senior vice president of human resource, Apple Computer, at a conference attended by six hundred technical employees. "Work" is "exertion or effort directed to produce or accomplish something" (one of fifty-three definitions in *Webster's Unabridged Encyclopedia Dictionary*). The definition supports Sullivan's advice. Networking requires effort, but the rewards are incalculable.

"Fifty percent of a manager's success is tied to the ability to network *effectively*," according to Hilliard Williams, vice president of Monsanto Chemical Group. "It goes beyond the grapevine; there is a higher level of consensus building that occurs in both internal and external networks."

There is a side benefit to networking as a career and lifestyle. Few jobs are etched in concrete; there are layoffs, firings, career changes, burnout, and midlife crises. Developing our contact base—both inside and outside of our industry—gives us some cushion. One never knows when the circumstances will occur that prompt us to explore other companies, industries or careers.

It may not even be for our own career changes that the business card file becomes important. A friend, relative or coworker may be in dire need of some leads. It could be that a chit we owe to a mentor, colleague or friend can be returned via our contact base. For me, that is often the best circumstance; when someone I know and/or owe is assisted by one of my markers, it feels good and is a good deed.

Play It Unsafe

There are people who don't, and won't, interact with others in a conscious networking effort. When asked why, the response was, "What if it doesn't work out?" If you don't try, there are no risks. The only problem is that there are also no rewards. "The biggest risk is not to risk. Taking risks is a necessity—playing it safe is dangerous and futile," claim Robert Kriegel and Louis Patler in *If It Ain't Broke, Break It!*[7]

We recommend someone for a job and it doesn't work out. I've done it, and apologized. There are a myriad of reasons it didn't work out, none of which were in my control or power. Would I recommend again? Absolutely.

Givers and Takers

Some of the people who don't and can't network are the super takers, who cannot *give* to others.[8] Some takers do give as long as it allows them to receive more. Sometimes they even "appear" to be givers, ready and willing to share resources, leads, and ideas. A colleague of mine once received this unfortunate description: "She has an upbeat personality, energy, an infectious laugh and convinces you that she is a friendly resource. Then you analyze your gut-level feeling and the situation and discover she has shared nothing and convinced you how lucky you are to work on her projects!"

Givers get taken and takers get to be given to. Be aware. Observe behavior and actions of others, determining if they either support or negate their words.

Networking at Its Finest

Being a good networker also means being a **visionary**—having the ability to see the larger picture of the future. We do things for people for no apparent reason or immediate return. "What goes around comes around" is a tenet of networking and of life.[9]

To have the process work, both personally and professionally, it must reflect certain values. To successfully do business via our contact base requires several current yet old-fashioned qualities, including a solid sense of ethics and a great degree of integrity. Current business literature has catapulted ethics, integrity, and honesty back into the limelight. A lot of us who are over forty are thrilled with the rediscovery of basic values.

Julian Monsarrat III, who works for the Marriott Corporation, embodies the ethical spirit of networking. "I treat people with respect, which is what I was taught to do. There's no magic, it's not a 'technique.' Just be nice to people. Most often you'll be treated the same way." Numerous networkers agreed that respecting people is the cornerstone of communication.

The Nineties Bottom Line

We all need to increase our networking know-how. It is no longer a gender issue; it is a people issue, and part and parcel of possessing savvy communications skills. The ability to create, support, and utilize a growing, overlapping, yet fluid base of referrals and resources requires style and substance. As John Naisbitt stated in *Megatrends,* "The old boy network is elitist; the new network is egalitarian—the information itself is the great equalizer."[10]

Networking enhances our lives. It includes and goes beyond the business card exchange. Above all, it is fun, and it works, if *you* will!

The first step is to assess our networks by taking stock of whom we know.

Reminders

➤ Network is now an action verb.
➤ Follow-up is the magic that makes the process of networking work.
➤ The closest thing to knowing something is to know where and how to find it.
➤ Powerful people have linkages that are plentiful, diverse, and expansive.
➤ A self-assessment of our skills and interests is critical for capturing confidence.
➤ Networking is a lifestyle of sharing resources, information, and ideas.
➤ Networking requires work—time, effort, and energy.
➤ Respect for people is the cornerstone of communication and networking in the nineties.

2

▶ ▶ ▶ ▶ ▶ ▶ ▶ ▶ ▶ ▶ ▶ ▶ ▶ ▶ ▶ ▶ ▶

The "Take Stock Exchange": It Ain't Know-How... It's Know-Who!

No, this is *not* the Boesky-Milken approach to insider trading. It's a perfectly legal assessment of your contact base which will produce a clear view of the potential connect-the-dots picture of your professional and personal networks.

A Seat on the Exchange

People who excel on the "Take Stock Exchange" have skill, experience, expertise, and a valid view of their networks. These people are the matchmakers. You call them asking for the name of a good graphic artist, agent, insurance broker, and in two minutes they can pull out a card from the Rolodex. The *know* who they know. They are aware of their multiple networks.

A recent article covered the New Age networking course...at a country club. These job-search strategies were being taught at the bastion of enclaves that traditionally kept people out. A new twist. The members of elite networks need assistance identifying their contact base, because they are the nouveau unemployed.

The increase in layoffs due to economic slowdowns, mergers and acquisitions, and business downsizing makes it mandatory to have our networks in place.

Know-How

We must have the skills, knowledge, and a track record. Education is important to a degree...or several degrees. Generally, that degree confirms that the bearer has expertise in a body of knowledge. I personally would prefer a surgeon who has the formal training, the degrees, *and* the experience. Although experience is a valid teacher, in many professions it is only part of the equation and does not supplant formal training.

Know-how is critical to job success. But it alone is not enough. There are many talented artists, musicians, and actors who do not get gallery showings, seats on the symphony, or parts in plays or movies. There are people who write both prolifically and well, and their unpublished novels and stories would make a bonfire big enough to heat Montana in midwinter.

©1982 Malcolm Hancock

Know-Who

There are thorough and knowledgeable tax accountants, law associates, and architects who do not make partner in their firms. You might know a person who falls into that category. You might even *be* that person: lots of know-how, little know-who. (It seems so darned unfair. But, that's life in the Big City.) Hard work, excellent work, is a pivotal part in the progress equation, but it is only a part. It is critical that we have a handle on the know-*who* portion of the equation.

Do you have three people at work whom you call cronies, associates, friends or coworkers? Whom do you talk to at the office? Is it only the people who can do something for you? Your peers? What about the secretaries? The custodians? Former colleagues? Competitors?

One of the few times we sit down to assess our contact base occurs during or after company layoffs (or midlife crises). That is not truly timely. Many of us are reluctant to reach out to our contacts lest we (1) appear needy, (2) be perceived as a user, or (3) have to return favors and, therefore, obligate ourselves to others.

Career counselors and outplacement firms strongly urge clients to identify their contacts. In my career consulting and workshop days, I wrote for and designed the *San Francisco Examiner* Career Series. I, too, charged people with this assessment task, and have not wavered from my belief in its importance.

As I was preparing to write this book, my situation prompted me to do the same. In planning my writing schedule, I had to plan "people" time. First, I assessed my needs, which were three: (1) to talk to close, loving friends, (2) to walk three to four miles daily as part of my aerobics regime, and (3) to associate with buddies with whom I am so comfortable that conversation, energy, and laughter flow effortlessly. After assessing my needs, I had to think hard.

Group 1 came to mind easily. These are the same friends that have been there forever. Group 2 had some new names, as did Group 3. And there was overlap among the groups. I had to be clear that no one on any of the lists could require any energy from me; there had to be a flow between us.

Who's On First?

It took time and required effort for me to take stock, but it was a good investment of my time (as it will be of yours). When the "writing Muse makes her exit," I have people to call who know my task at hand and who have encouraged me to call. They are truly a support network, much needed in the solitary process of writing.

What's On Second?

I recommend that you, too, build a network. To prepare: Glance at your address book, business card file, professional directories, softball team roster, Christmas card list. Please don't groan, get annoyed or disappointed—trust me on this! Those of you who are computer people may have a software program to use as a format, but you must produce and process as well as "word-process" the names.

The rest of us should get a three-ring binder or notebook, loose-leaf lined paper, and a favorite writing instrument. Mine is a #2 pencil with a superior eraser. Now I sound like a teacher—even to me.

Weave Your Web

Life is like a cobweb,
not an organization chart.
—H. Ross Perot

List the categories on page 24, one per sheet. You may have to get a refill of paper. Why so many diverse categories that seem unimportant for our careers? Because there are too many stories of leads from unexpected sources. Some names can appear in several categories because networks overlap. You may also want to identify your baseball and ballet buddies, movie mavens, and comedy club cronies. If you have other categories to consider, add a sheet for each.

- Continue to add to your list. Binders are useful that way. We know lots of people. Some names can appear in several categories; our networks are multifaceted; we are in numerous networks, some of which may overlap.
- Place the lists together on the table or floor.
- Draw lines from name to name between categories. Links and lines connect the dots.
- Take your card file and add to the various lists. This is an ongoing process. If there are cards of people about whom you are clueless, toss them. We do have to know whom we know.

If you were fired or laid off today, you now know whom you would call. Most people like helping the people they know and like! By having your network assessed, you'd know whom to call if you were named chairman of the high school reunion committee or the local March of Dimes gourmet gala. You also know what or who is missing.

The Gaps: Fill in the Blanks

This process also reveals the gaps—what is missing from our network and life. If we are aware of our needs and goals, we can begin to fill in the blanks. When I left teaching and started my speaking business, I joined Women Entrepreneurs. As my business grew, and I needed to increase my small-business skills, I joined the San Francisco Chamber of Commerce and became an active volunteer in the Small Business Department (on the Education Committee, of course). My

Identify Base of Contacts

Identification of your base of contacts is critical. Get a clear picture of whom you know. Use card files, Christmas list, old address books, alumni associations, membership lists, telephone records, the Little League list.

People in Position to Influence	People Who Know Others	Coworkers/ Former Coworkers	Clients/ Former Clients	Colleagues/ Competitors
Family/ Ex-family/ Extended Family	Neighbors/ Former Neighbors	Classmates/ Alumni	Associates From Organizations, Charity, Church, Synagogue	Special Interest Groups (Golf, Health Club, Bridge Buddies)

Networking is a personal process which links us to others and enriches our professional and personal lives. It is based on an exchange of leads, advice, support, information, and time.

Some Categories and People to Consider

PERSONAL

Family
Ex-family
Friends
Professional
• Doctor
• Dentist
• CPA
• Manicurist
• Barber
• Mechanic
Neighbors
Ex-neighbors
Bowling team

Relatives of:
• Friends
• Relatives
• Colleagues
Friends of:
• Relatives
• Friends
• Colleagues
Sports friends
Parents of friends of your children
Church or synagogue
Bridge buddies

PROFESSIONAL

Coworkers
Bosses
Subordinates
Clients
Ex-clients
Colleagues
Associates
Alumni

Competitors
Politicians
Classmates:
• Grammar school
• High school
• College
• Religious school

membership in the National Speakers Association reduced my learning curve in my chosen field. The release of my first book, *How to Work a Room,* necessitated the addition of the world of publishing and writing; now I subscribe to *Publishers Weekly* and am a member of the Authors Guild.

The Other Part of the Principle

Having know-how is important, as is know-who. "It's not what you know, but who you know that counts" is a familiar phrase. Growing up in Chicago somehow made me a true believer. The payments were so tough if you didn't get it.

The late Sally Livingston, my "femtor," gave me a lifelong wake-up call when she was teaching techniques of networking in the San Francisco Bay Area in the early 1980s. She explained, "We are aware that it is not *what* you know, but *who* you know that counts. More importantly, it is *who knows you!*" Words of wisdom that impacted my business, my writing, and my perspective. It made sense and gave a structure to this whole process of making contacts and being connected...and, in fact, just *being.* The *"a-ha!"** so loudly struck a chord that it continues to resonate and to guide me over a decade later.

Who knows you? If you call a local politician, is your call returned? If the marching band needs money for new uniforms, can you pull a committee together to fund-raise? Does the business editor of your hometown paper treat you as a resource? Does she even know you? Does the president of your professional association know you? Respond to your suggestions?

A Giant Coup

In October of 1987 the San Francisco Giants were in the play-offs. My friend, Chicago attorney David Schultz, an avid Cubs fan, was visiting and challenged me: "Susan, we'll see how good your network is...if you can pull off tickets for the play-offs." Who could resist? I went through the card file and

*See Glossary.

hit the phones and managed to get us upper box seats on the first-base line from an old political crony who had resurfaced in my new network. Because we had stayed in touch periodically, I scored! (The Giants didn't do as well.)

Sometimes we "get known" by our relationship to others:

"Hello! I'm Kirk Douglas, Michael's dad."
"Hello! I am Mr. Boynton, a colleague of Miss Brooks."
"Hello! I am Pam Martens, Joyce Siegel's daughter, the teacher."
"Hi! I'm Shelly Berger, Susan's cousin."

These introductions are relational and help us to establish a connection so important to the "Take Stock Exchange." Once we have taken stock of our networks, we can continue to use our business card files to stay in touch with our contacts.

Reminders

➤ It is important to have *know-how*. Skill and experience are key.

➤ It is equally important to have *know-who*.

➤ The "Take Stock Exchange" is an assessment of our entire contact base.

➤ Identification of our personal and professional networks is crucial. Use paper and pencil (or your computer) and start writing.

➤ Identify the gaps in your network and fill them in.

➤ The current massive layoffs are forcing people at all levels in the workplace to stay visible. It is even more important in turbulent times that people know you!

➤ The time spent identifying your base of contacts is an investment in your success and the success of others with whom you share your resources.

3

▶ ▶ ▶ ▶ ▶ ▶ ▶ ▶ ▶ ▶ ▶ ▶ ▶ ▶ ▶ ▶ ▶ ▶ ▶ ▶

It's in the Cards

If networking is a lifestyle (and it is), then business cards are the lifesavers…timesavers. Business cards are today's version of the calling cards of yesteryear, which were also communication tools. Our business cards say something about who we are, what we do, and where we can be reached. The manner in which we handle the distribution and collection of business cards speaks volumes about us, our style, and our knowledge of business card etiquette.

Caveat: The following information is geared to business in the United States.

Breaching Business Card Etiquette

I have been regaled with tales of horror involving the handling of business cards, including that of a fellow who attended an event, arrived after everyone was seated, and placed his card in front of each attendee, said a few words, and then left the event.

Events—be they reunions, meetings, conferences, fundraisers, or parties—are opportunities to meet people and exchange cards…*after* an exchange of conversation, *not instead of it*. Will this "card shark" be remembered? Most likely, but not pleasantly. Will he receive any follow-up calls or referrals? Unlikely.

There are some who hand out a business card as soon as they disengage from the initial handshake. That is a school of thought to which I do not subscribe. While that allows you to examine the card, it interrupts a potential conversation by taking the focus off the person and placing it on an inanimate object: The Business Card. To reiterate: The business card is exchanged as the follow-up to an exchange of words that establishes communication, support, and mutual interest—not self-interest.

How we handle our exchange of business cards reflects the *hard-sell* versus *soft-sell* approach. Most people prefer the soft-sell approach, which indicates interest in them as an individual, not as someone who can do something for you. Because people communicate with people, not with cards, this approach applies even in formalized networking clubs, where the exchange of business cards is part of the agenda.

The business card gives people a tangible way to remember you and to contact you. Again, how we handle the collection and distribution of our cards determines whether or not people would want to do either.

It's in the Cards

1. Business Cards by Design

Make sure the design of your card does not obscure the most important information (which should always be kept current). To avoid card clutter, your company logo should not be so large that the information has to be set too small to be easily read. I learned that I needed bifocals when I was handed a card that appeared to have no phone number on it.

According Mollyanne Maremaa, graphic designer, "The design of the card has to be clean so that the important information is easily discernible. The most important information is the bearer's name, then the phone number, then company name. Some people feel the fax number should be listed last, but the last position on the card is visually the easiest to read, so use it for the phone number."[11]

Make sure your card fits into either a business card file or a Rolodex™. Oversized cards, folded cards, or cards that are designed vertically are attention-getting because they're different, "but that difference may not best facilitate follow-up as the horizontally designed cards will do," Maremaa advises. "Remember that the purpose of the card is to provide a formal introduction that indicates legitimacy. A card is *not* a catalog of goods and services."

2. Devise a Card Carrying and Collection System

"Use a right or left pocket for handing out cards and the other pocket for collecting," advises Esta Swig, San Francisco attorney. "It eliminates the embarrassment of giving out the business card of the person you just met."

Many business card cases are stunning and make a powerful accessory statement. But if they are thin, the additional statement is, "My card-carrying capacity is limited." Choose a card holder that is useful and attractive. I use a red leather cigarette case.

3. Avoid "Sticky" Situations

It's awkward to reach for a card after indulging in sweet-and-sour chicken. Do you suck the sauce off your fingers so it doesn't get on the cards? Or leave it there? What a dilemma! Do your nibbling and noshing* first; then circulate, converse, and exchange business cards. Better yet, eat before you go and avoid a sticky situation.

4. Mnemonic Devices

Write a mnemonic device on the other person's card that will help you remember that person. Do so as soon as

*See Glossary

possible, but not in his or her presence. It could be an observation you made about a unique tie, a pair of cuff links or earrings, or a shared interest in hockey, comedy clubs, baseball or ballet. Because we are often on information overload, such a notation jogs our memory.

The notation on several of the cards in my file is "Rancho" for Rancho La Puerta, the health spa where I have met a number of interesting people. Where we met is the common area of interest and a basis for conversation; for example, "Have you been back to the Ranch?" "How did you like the aerobics instructor?" "Are you still sneaking in M&M's and diet soda?"

Several years ago I met Allen Teshima, a rep for Du Pont, in a program I gave in Hawaii. We have been friends ever since, because we both remembered our first exchange and notations on each other's card. Oddly enough, in checking with him, I learned we remembered totally different comments. Allen remembers my saying, "Oh, you work for Du Pont; you make my panty hose," as I looked at my legs to check for runs. I remember that we both walked out of our respective rooms in the Oahu hotel, where the conference was held, at the same time. Allen smiled and said, "Adjoining rooms!" (We had a good laugh comparing the notations that served as our memory joggers!)

Harvey Mackay, author of two books on the *New York Times* best-seller list and a successful business person, believes that "once you write it [important information] down...you know where you can find it again."[12]

5. Bring Enough Cards

Granted, if there are nine hundred people at the Chamber of Commerce Business Exchange, as the one I once attended in Honolulu, you obviously won't carry that many business cards. Nor should you. In the course of a two-hour reception, it would be unlikely that you would (or could) converse with more than twenty-five people.

6. Be Prepared

Always have business cards with you, a few extra in your wallet, glove compartment, and briefcase. We never know whom we'll run into and where. It might even happen on the jogging path, at the barbershop, or at your cousin's wedding. But also be appropriate; exercise judgement. Distribution at funerals is tasteless.

7. Don't Play "Card Games." Be Wary of Those Who Do

After a conversation at a business reception I asked a fellow, "Do you have a card?" He looked at me deadpan and said, "Yes." He stood there making no move to get one. After what seemed to be an interminably long time, I asked, "May I have one?" "Of course," he replied. I was very uncomfortable, but felt compelled to ask him why he didn't give me his card initially. "That is not the question you asked; you asked if I *had* a card, not if you could have it." Yikes! I was never—and am still not—good at card games, be it blackjack, gin rummy, or those involving business cards.

While most people will ask for your card in return, some won't. There are two ways to handle this: Either offer your card after you have collected theirs, or send a note and include your card.

If the person refuses to give you a card or has run out, you may offer one of yours to jot down the information.

There is a card game that has been brought to my attention because it has been shared as a power strategy in seminars. Perhaps under the umbrella of power plays and card games, attendees have been advised not to carry their cards or not to give them to people. Instead, they collect cards, therefore having control over the contacts and follow-up. Ostensibly, they are then in the more powerful position.

Creating a contact base of resources requires that those

people who would and could be resources, clients, referrals, or friends are treated with respect, not like a throwaway card. Powerful, successful people are generally well bred, well mannered, and well intentioned.

8. Devise a Card "Container" System

Be it a business card file, Rolodex™, or shoe box, use whatever works best for you. I use oblong business card files. Once I return from an event and call or send a note, I clip the cards together, identify the event, organization, and date, and I "live with" the cards for a while...before I file them.

One is never too young to start. My friend Esta Swig was stunned when her seven-year-old son, David, wanted a Lucite business card file he saw in a store. "David, you're only seven. Why do you want a business card file?" "I need it to keep the cards I collect when I go to the auto shows with Dad!" (Martin Swig owns Autocenter in San Francisco.)

David, who also collects coins, rocks, and miniature cars, has organized those collections well, too. David has already been involved in a school fund-raising project for which he used his business card collection of Mom and Dad's friends and associates. This is the nineties and David Swig, at the age of seven, is prepared and organized. (I did buy two of his school calendars!)

A card file can become overstocked. In chapter 13 you'll learn how to clean it out, which is as important as expanding it.

Computer Networks

Business cards are the information tools we need to continue our communication and follow-up with people we meet. There are several software programs for the computer networker that may be useful. A computer industry magazine or your local computer store will have the latest information.

A word of caution: The ability to network is a "people" skill, not a technical one. Technology only enhances, not replaces.

After a speech to the radio and record industry, "Joe," a record person, related how he used his computer software program to input business cards, data on the contact, and an on-line tickler system. "When I call one of the radio guys, I have the names of the wife and kids and notes from our last conversation—which I throw in." As a noncomputer person, it sounded impressive if not magical to me. But I added, "Remember, this is a person-to-person communication."

That evening in the hospitality suite, a radio producer confirmed Joe's story. "Yes, he certainly has his computer rap together, and as far as I am concerned, it's jive. Joe calls and talks to me like I am his long-lost buddy, so I'll add his records to our playlist. He knows so much about me and our last conversation. Then, one day, I returned his call, clearly stating my name to my 'buddy.' His response was incredible, he was totally disoriented. He had no clue who I was, nor did he know anything about me without his software program on his screen. When he finally did 'call me up' on his screen, he had shown his true colors."

We want to be remembered, but not manipulated.

Don't Foul Up: Follow-Up!

The Magic of Making Your Network: Follow-up. I often get teased by a colleague because I send notes and call to chat. His implication is that he is too busy in his marketing for such "idle" tasks. Building a network of contacts, resources, colleagues, and friends requires actions that take time. Harvey Mackay advises us to "consider it an investment." What becomes of that investment (in meeting people) "if I don't follow through? It's down the drain unless I organize and make use of it."[13]

Establishing relationships takes time, from the moment you enter a room to mingle and meet people, to when you return to your office, to the follow-up that you will do. Take the cards you have collected and read them, pay attention to the mnemonic devices you have noted, try to visualize the person. Jot down any additional information on the card, on an index card, or add it to your software program. Then pick the people you want to contact:

1. **Send a note.** One sentence will do: handwritten. Computer-generated may be more efficient, but pen on good paper is memorable. Perhaps you learned that Roger is a hockey fan and you found an article comparing hockey to business management. Send the article with one of the following notes:

Informal:

> Roger,
>
> Enjoyed meeting you at the awards banquet,
>
> Best,
>
> Groucho Marks

Please only say so if it is true.

Semiformal:

> Roger,
>
> Saw this after our conversation at the business banquet. Thought you might find this to be of interest.
>
> Regards,
>
> Groucho Marks

Formal:

> Dear Roger,
>
> *I was pleased that we had an opportunity to speak at last night's benefit. Your work sounds very intriguing. Perhaps we can get together for lunch upon your return from the Far East.*
>
> *Sincerely,*
>
> *Groucho Marks*

2. **Call within twelve to fourteen days of mailing the note.** Have three optional days to offer for a breakfast or lunch. If you don't connect with Roger, leave a specific message reminding him of where you met and a conversation jog. If you get to leave a voice-mail message, be sure to reflect interest and a smile in your voice.

3. **Do not send your brochure.** Unless Roger requested it, do not send your company's press kit or annual report. If he did, then do so promptly.

4. **Wait twelve to fourteen days and call.** Let's say Roger did request your company information and hasn't returned your follow-up call. Wait two weeks and call again. (Messages do get lost and garbled.)

We will not connect with every person we meet, nor should we expect that every contact works out.

The follow-up reflects respect for the other person's time lines and schedules. Respect is the core of any contact that may, with time and trust, blossom into an established relationship. Wait a couple of months. Send a column, cartoon, lead, information about an upcoming event, or card. I have fun at various holidays sending notes of good wishes or cards for the occasion.

Reminders

➤ Business cards are the information tools for the networking process. They are used to follow up a conversation, not to replace it.

➤ Be sure your cards are designed to be read easily.

➤ Distribute and collect with care and consideration. A well-designed card deserves the most appropriate manner of distribution.

➤ Write mnemonic devices on cards to jog your memory.

➤ Bring enough cards and always have them with you.

➤ Don't play card games or power plays. Cards are used to enhance follow-up, not to get positioned on a game board.

➤ Use technology, don't abuse it.

➤ Organize the cards to facilitate follow-up.

➤ Follow up, Follow up, Follow up ... with notes, calls, articles, cartoons, leads.

4

▶ ▶ ▶ ▶ ▶ ▶ ▶ ▶ ▶ ▶ ▶ ▶ ▶ ▶ ▶ ▶ ▶

Visibility Value

Being Seen

"Go out! You'll never meet anyone sitting at home" (or at your desk or in your office). These words of advice, which have a nuance of nagging and sound slightly familiar, are on target. We cannot create a positive presence unless we are present. We can stay in touch by letter, phone, fax, or E-mail, but a face-to-face conversation establishes rapport like no other interaction or communication. That is the basis for the most productive relationships.

"Going out" is the first step to creating visibility. It is difficult to leave a project, a deadline, piles of urgent files, clients, patients, or customers to attend a professional meeting, community luncheon, or business event. Yes, attending an event with strangers is our number one most uncomfortable situation (public speaking is number two), validated by a *USA Today* Reader Poll.[14]

As jazz musician Art Blakey said, "If you're not appearing, you are disappearing."

I wrote *How to Work a Room* to provide a commonsense

guide for savvy socializing. If entering a room full of people, especially strangers, is a source of discomfort, I urge you to read it.

Ten Tips from the Mingling Maven

Magnificent Minglers:

1. Possess the ability to make others feel comfortable
2. Appear to be confident and at ease
3. Have an ability to laugh at themselves (not at others)
4. Show interest in others; they maintain eye contact, self-disclose, ask questions, and actively listen
5. Extend themselves to others; they lean into a greeting with a firm handshake and a smile
6. Convey a sense of energy and enthusiasm—a joie de vivre
7. Are well-rounded, well-informed, well-intentioned, and well-mannered.
8. Prepare vignettes or stories of actual occurrences that are interesting, humorous, and appropriate
9. Introduce people to each other with an infectious enthusiasm (there is *no* other kind) that motivates conversation between the introducees
10. Convey respect and genuinely like people—the core of communicating

If we are more comfortable at events, and we can be, we develop a positive presence that is memorable.

On the Scene

There are three arenas in which visibility contributes to professional viability:

- Intra-company (Phase I)
- Professional Associations (Phase II)
- Community Organizations (Phase III)

Phase I—Intra-company

Whether you commute to an office or telecommute, it is important to stay visible, according to career consultant James Challenger.[15] And according to Paul Stern, multinational corporate CEO, "It is useful to belong to a network within a company...which consists of people with whom you trade information."[16] Being seen allows one to have the casual conversation that is the cornerstone of relationships.

Can You "Spare" One Strike Against You?

Yes, I mean the bowling team! A former Fighting Illini of my acquaintance bowls on a division team for his Fortune 500 company. Nothing interferes with his Tuesday nights at the alley. The camaraderie that develops off-duty during shared activities makes the workplace more enjoyable. It allows us to have a network of coworkers from other departments or divisions in the company, which increases our information base and effectiveness ratings.

It is not enough to just do a job well; people have to know who we are. James Challenger suggests that we keep tabs on special office events and attend the functions.

The Company Picnic: It Can Be One!

A three-legged race may not be your idea of a good time, but the willingness to be in one, and to have fun doing so, contributes to your visibility and being perceived as a good sport. If everyone is tied in a sack, there is no loss of dignity if you are similarly accessorized.

Talk to everyone: coworkers, spouses, and kids. The weather, always a concern at a picnic, is a good place to start. And favorite foods, favorite activity, the location of the picnic, its accessibility and setting, are also good conversation starters.

Sign up to be on a committee that makes you a "host" and visible. We were all taught good host skills—to see to other people's comfort. In case the picnic in the preserves is driving everyone buggy, carry a can of Bug-Off and offer the unprotected a shpritz.* That will make you memorable!

Treat the spouses as the interesting individuals they are. Anything less could come back to haunt you. In the nineties, most spouses have their own jobs, careers, businesses, or community volunteer work, or all of these. Some are even men!

I gave a speech on "How to Work a Room" for two hundred spouses of CEOs of mid-sized banks. One woman shared her experience: "My husband's senior vice president treats me as though I am of no consequence. Who does he think has the boss's ear when we drive to visit our son in college or enjoy a quiet supper at home? What a fool! Which I have mentioned to my husband at several timely intervals."

Kid Conversation

At casual company events, offspring are often included, and structured games, contests, and activities are offered for them. Talk to the kids of your coworkers, colleagues, and superiors. They go to school, have favorite subjects, sports, activities, interests, homework, and projects. If shown interest, they will respond. Ignoring kids makes a negative statement; paying attention to them makes a positive one, which may hold you in good stead.

Phase II—Professional Associations

Maximize on Memberships

It takes more than membership dues to be visible in your professional associations. Writing a check and filling out the information card will get you on the roster. That is not enough, and does not contribute to your network of contacts.

You could cold-call other members or send a mailer, but

*See Glossary.

if people don't know you, it's a crapshoot. However, if you attend a percentage of meetings, work the cocktail hour, sign up on a committee, or volunteer for a special project, you will become better known.

We often hear of incidents where people did not do as they said they would, when they said they would. And such behavior makes for indelible memories. You have to do a thorough, timely, effective job, especially as a volunteer.

It serves no purpose to volunteer for a committee, or run for an office, and then do a poor job. It is far better to understand that volunteer work for any organization requires our best. If we do not demonstrate excellence and commitment, we can expect to be nixed for any possible job referrals from our committee cohorts. People do talk and don't recommend known screwups. We all know that, but it bears repeating.

RoAne's Remedial Rules

Always do your best whether for pay or for intrinsic rewards. The opportunity to meet people on committees is an excellent one. "Consider every contact to be the beginning of a long-term relationship, because things do change and it helps to be remembered well," advises Jim Cathcart, speaker and author of *Relationship Selling*.

Pick a committee and project in an area of interest. If the fund-raiser interests you, do it. If you have no desire, skill, or interest in writing, don't volunteer for the newsletter committee. If you like dealing with hacks and flacks, sign up on the public relations committee.

Résumé Add-ons

A position in a professional organization is an excellent way to add to your résumé, especially if the position is one that utilizes skills and experiences that are different from those used in your job.

Once you have successfully implemented these programs and utilized your skills, they are marketable. When I joined the National Speakers Association, I signed up to be on the publicity committee. I had demonstrated my public relations skills early in my business when I wrote for the *San Francisco Examiner* Business Careers Series. My participation on that committee enabled me to refine and expand those skills.

Even though I have since hired a public relations professional for my speaking engagements and books, I still like doing it. So I volunteered to be on the publicity committee for the "Race for the Cure," sponsored by the Susan Komen Foundation for Breast Cancer Research. It feels good to contribute skills, which I refined in my professional organization, for a worthy cause that I support.

Never Know Whom You'll Run Into (Dangling Participle Apologies)

Being visible in our professional organizations requires a thoughtful image assessment. *RoAne's Law:* The worse you look running into the market for a carton of milk, the more important to your career is the person whom you did *not* want to see you looking that bad. In the supermarket, the hardware store, or on the running track, we are cut some slack. But not at the monthly meeting of the Association of Image Consultants.

How we dress, accessorize, and behave speaks volumes. Our business cards project our image, and our demeanor determines how we are perceived. "Acting appropriately" is the phrase that is the guidepost for getting along in situations. How we act at a ballet is different than at a baseball game. Some people have a clear understanding of situational differences of being appropriate, and others have none. It has to do with the manner in which we present and carry ourselves, what we communicate, and how we do so. And that manner we project can serve to enhance us in our networks, or to sever us from them.

The Challenge of Change

As positions change, moving from manager to executive, so do the associations and organizations to be joined. According to Paul Stern, "People at a higher level will join...Conference Board or National Chamber of Commerce. At the national level there are certain industry-wide clubs which are key to networking such as the Electrical Manufacturers Club...members refrain from talking about business except in general terms. It's ideal for senior executives in the industry to establish relationships with each other."[17]

We do have to move on and to change in our affiliations as our positions and careers change. It may be uncomfortable to do so but it is necessary (see chapter 13).

How to Be a Chamber Made

Again, it is not enough to be just a dues-paying member. Granted, a listing in the Chamber of Commerce directory affords one visibility, but that visibility is exponentially increased by the presence of you or your employees on the various volunteer committees. Each chamber has numerous volunteer opportunities. For smaller businesses and sole proprietorships, being involved ensures visibility.

Several of the people who served on the Education Committee with me nine years ago are now on the board of directors; one was president last year. They worked their way up through chamber channels and they worked hard and well to achieve visibility.

Lemon Suckers Are Just That

Practice the Ten Tips from the Mingling Maven. Be a person whom people want to be around.

Woody Allen said it best: "Eighty percent of life is just showing up." Take a risk—go! But wherever you go to be visible, always go with an agenda: that of having a good time. People are attracted to people who are having fun, and that's the truth.

When was the last time you attended a professional luncheon, spotted a member in the corner frowning, and thought, "That's someone I'd like to get to know"? The answer most likely is never. People are open to a person whose face, posture, and eyes invite communication. The stance that is open and relaxed, the face with a smile, a head slightly tilted, reflect approachability.[18]

Phase III—Community Organizations

Creating a Community Presence

Each one of us has issues that are near and dear to our hearts. Involvement in those areas feels good to us because we are doing our share to make a difference. In my first life I was a teacher. While the monetary rewards were minimal (nobody ever chooses teaching for the money), the intrinsic rewards were incalculable.

There were many times that mutiny or murder felt like viable options, but then there was the day that one student finally understood long division (or algorithms, or use of quotation marks, or how to play a bar in a minor key). There is nothing like seeing that magical light turn on and the glow illuminate the face of the student who finally "got it."

Serving our community interests is an opportunity to do just that. We are afforded the opportunity to meet people with whom we already share a common bond, to work side by side for a reward that is not monetary.

Meet By-products

There are numerous nonprofit agencies that are looking for knowledgeable, talented people willing to commit their time, energy, and expertise.

We can serve on boards, participate in projects, or attend sponsored events. The by-product is that we meet people, gain visibility, and increase our networks, resources, and business. It happens informally when people know who we are and what we do, and are comfortable with our capabilities.

My buddy Landy Eng had asked me to join the board of the Career Resource Development Center, which has provided career, language, and job training for over twenty-five years. Two weeks earlier, Carl LaMell, my business "boss," suggested that I get involved in a nonprofit agency. "Susan, you are a home-based entrepreneur and writer, two very solitary endeavors. You need to be part of a group with formal meetings, subcommittee projects, and places that you *have* to be that have nothing to do with your speaking or writing." For two years I worked with a cross section of talented, bright, energetic men and women on the CRDC board. I learned a lot and had a chance to share my ideas and support with an agency that is doing good works. But I relearned that structured meetings are not my forte. I was reminded of being in school as a child, being forced to sit in my seat and be quiet, and not to chat with my classmates. And later, as a teacher, being forced to sit in faculty meetings, to be quiet and not to chat with my colleagues. Striking similarities! Leopards, including this one, do not change their spots, unless we decide to endure physical, emotional or psychological dermabrasion.

Meet By-products and Hire Authority

The University of Illinois Foundation's National Leadership Network has a San Francisco Bay Area chapter. Serving on it has been interesting because we are all Fighting Illini and, yet, are a diverse group. One of our alumni, Con Hewitt, the local managing partner of Ernst & Young, called and said, "Susan, we want you to give a speech on your book *How to Work a Room*. And, by the way, I want about one hundred copies of it." Did Con want to see a press kit? No. References? No. A video? No. He knew me and after working with me knew I would do my best. That's all he needed.

Attending our annual Women Entrepreneur awards breakfast is always special. Last year I met two staff members for the March of Dimes, which piqued my interest, having been on the first Mothers' March in the fifties. They asked me to chair an event: a "Jail and Bail" fund-raiser. What fun! And a lot of work.

I went through my card file and called our San Francisco deputy chief of investigations, Frank Reed. He sent me a sample warrant so that we could mimic the language of arrests to appear "authentic." The day of the event, our supportive "prisoners" were whisked away to a luncheon. And there I met two women, sitting at different tables, who have since become my good friends. One Saturday night I danced at one's wedding, and hope to do the same for the other soon.

Your community has numerous agencies that rely on volunteer assistance. Community involvement contributes to our visibility, which can help us make business, make sense, and make friends! So go out and volunteer.

As we gain visibility and become more politically savvy, we can start "managing our markers."

Reminders

➤ Before joining organizations, read their brochures, reports, and newsletters.

➤ Attend two meetings before you join, to see if it's a fit.

➤ Know *why* you have joined and how that membership fits into your professional plans or personal preference.

➤ Introduce yourself to officers, staff, and other members of the association or organization.

➤ Join committees, be active.

➤ Attend special events.

➤ Work rooms.

➤ Write articles for the newsletter/journal.

➤ Give presentations in your area of expertise to the organization.

➤ Join the board of a community agency.

➤ Perform at your best as a volunteer.

➤ Let people know what you do, but know that is incidental.

➤ Above all, have a good time; bring along your light-hearted laughter and you will be a standout!

5

▶ ▶ ▶ ▶ ▶ ▶ ▶ ▶ ▶ ▶ ▶ ▶ ▶ ▶ ▶ ▶ ▶

Paying Up
Pays Off

In the musical *Evita,* one of the generals defines politics as "the art of the possible." A keen sense of business politics or savvy can dramatically impact one's career. Not having that savvy also impacts one's career, networks, and life—negatively.

A Timely Timesaver

Too often, people are overheard complaining about the politics of a situation, claiming that "I just want to do my job well." Let me share a timesaving tip: *Waste not one moment lamenting about the horrible politics in your office or organization.* There is no gathering of three or more persons free of politics. Just remember the last family holiday reunion you attended. (Maybe you'd rather not!)

Too many of us separate our skills as professionals from those needed to compete, to create, and to collaborate politically. There are specific abilities and skills required of every job, but the benefit of heightened political skill and the awareness of how any organization, corporation, formal or informal network operates, who operates it, the written policies, and the *unwritten* rules contribute to our effectiveness.

Political Savvy Secures Success

The term "politics" has always conjured up an image of the cigar-chomping, deal-making, sleazy character who buys and sells used cars and/or people. Due to that image, many of us grow up thinking that politics is a dirty word. After many years as a public school teacher in Chicago and San Francisco, I can assure you that politics is *not* an invective for which we sent students to the principal's office.

Many people blame politics for loss of positions, promotions, and career mobility. It is convenient to do so and prevents us from having to assess our actions and behaviors or the lack of such. But political business savvy is a critical quality that bears attention. Without it, one will lack awareness of the players, the written and understood policies, and the way the organization operates. If we aren't savvy, our resources may, like the water in the California drought, dry up. But political savvy is the water that nourishes the planted seeds and makes them grow.

In Search of Red-Tape Cutters

We all want to be perceived as people who can get things done. The authors of *In Search of Excellence,* Tom Peters and Robert Waterman, mention that those who can cut red tape are valued. I have never heard anyone complain about politics who is a pro at it or who had been the beneficiary of some savvy actions.

A benefit of heightened political skill is an awareness as well as a grasp of how things are done and who makes things happen. Most of us want to be around those "doers" and, in fact, be one ourselves.

Good Networkers Get Things Done

"Call Joe. If he can't help you fix your problem, he knows who can," is a compliment. Whether you are a cop or corporate executive, having a network of resources helps get the job done. "Earlier in my career, I was a SWAT team member and leader, and we often worked with other police departments and the FBI. We developed friendships," shared Frank Reed, deputy chief of investigations, San Francisco Police Department. "Now that we are older, and are less likely to be jumping off roofs, we are in administration and my FBI counterparts are in surveillance. I pick up the phone, call my buddy from the FBI, and we get their assistance ASAP, and we catch criminals quicker. We do the same for them; it works both ways."

The Five Fatal Flaws

The drawbacks to your professional life for not having political savvy are clear. Your boss, colleagues, and coworkers may perceive you as:

1. Missing a critical skill
2. Lacking awareness and finesse
3. Not being a team player or a good networker
4. Lacking in common sense (which is really uncommon). This umbrella term has come to encompass logic, practicality, savvy, and know-how
5. Untrustworthy of confidences and critical information

"Politics" by Definition

I, too, lose sight of the pervasiveness of the politics of a situation for which I expect a logical definition. My friend Jean Miller, a successful salesperson, reminded me of that when I wondered out loud why a certain business magazine would feature information about "working rooms" and ignore my first book when they had copies on hand. "Susan, it's politics; you'll never know the truth; just let it go and move on." So I did, thanks to Jean's reminder—and didn't renew my subscription! That's politics, too.

"Politics is a process for getting things done...[where] everyone barters for favors," according to Marilyn Moats Kennedy in *Office Politics: Seizing Power, Wielding Clout.*[19] Understandably, that allows us to move forward in our positions, professions, and formal and informal networks. Yes, one hand washes the other. Did you ever try washing just one hand?

Here are some ideas for developing your sense of business politics:

- Observe your colleagues, subordinates, and supervisors. Who eats with whom? Works out together? Commutes together?
- Read the body language of your coworkers as names, projects, and assignments are mentioned.
- Listen to conversations in the elevators, staff rooms, nearby restaurants, and even the washrooms.
- Converse with your coworkers, clients, colleagues, and competitors.

There is another critical career tool that fits under the umbrella of business politics. When it exists, it is viewed as awareness coupled with positive action. When it is missing, a career can be damaged by the perceived lack of know-how. The behavior described is the awareness of reciprocity and the willingness to reciprocate.

Reciprocity Rules

Reciprocity is the cornerstone of networking. It is a common courtesy, the give-and-take that is the glue that makes things stick together. Giving without expectation may work in some instances. Not giving back does not.

Reciprocity is a very basic behavior, crucial to business careers and to personal lives. I have heard tales of unsavory, unpolitic people who are the takers. They never acknowledge what they receive—time, advice, clients, contacts, leads or gifts—let alone trade back. It is as if the "me generation" mentality has permeated and devastated the area once known as basic common courtesy. But we are in the nineties and a more solid mind-set is catching on. Reciprocity is a courtesy and a critical career skill. If one chooses not to value, acknowledge, and trade back, when possible, one must be prepared to suffer the consequences.

In the speaking business where speakers' bureaus take twenty-five to thirty percent of the fee, it is not uncommon to acknowledge a referral with a ten percent fee. "Sally," a colleague of mine, recommended another speaker, "Jane," to a contract with a Fortune 500 company. When Sally called to tell Jane, she clearly stated that her policy is to pay ten percent. Unfortunately, Sally had already given Jane's phone number to the client. Jane said, "We don't pay fees; it's too hard to track!" How odd! Jane speaks about organization skills. My friend received a computer-generated form letter, no promised reciprocal referral, no fee, no token of thanks. Jane got a $50,000 contract. The word is out on Jane.

Once again, if you have time to receive help, favors, gifts, advice; you would be wise to make the time to give acknowledgement, which is a common courtesy. If not, your sources of support could dry up. People do talk, the word gets out, and writers get great material.

In *Straight to the Top,* Paul Stern unequivocally states that "courtesy must be the guiding principle behind actions you take.... Courtesy is not an affectation, it is a *mirror of character*."[20] One good turn does deserve another.

Managing the Markers

Being from Chicago has contributed to my awareness, viewpoint, and understanding in certain matters. There are times when I feel that I am in a scene from one of my all-time favorite movies, *Guys and Dolls* (the 1992 Broadway remake, which won four Tony Awards). No, I am not Miss Adelaide, the chorus girl, nor Sister Sarah, the Salvation Army angel. I hear myself sounding like Big Jule, the Boss of the Chicago "organization," explaining that Sky Masterson is "holding my markers." In the movie, these markers were a gambling debt paid up by attending a Salvation Army meeting. But Big Jule knew that he took the gamble, played the game, and lost...and that he now owed Sky Masterson. It's simple, the clear-cut rules of the game. Play, Lose, Owe—or, for my purposes— Play, *Use,* Owe.

Being in the business world, having a career, growing a business or entering a profession are also a gamble. You enter the game; there are stakes (and much at stake); you learn the rules and the culture; you're dealt a hand. Play your cards right! Work hard and well, and your business gains; you move up the career ladder and your professional expertise and status increase.

1-15

Sorry, this is the ladder to the electrical system.
The ladder to success is down the hall.

One—No Trump

There are times we feel that the deck is stacked against us, and sometimes we can stack the deck in our favor. How do we do this? By being savvy. Having a sense of people—an understanding of human nature—people skills, if you please. My friend of three decades, Carl LaMell, exemplifies "savvy." He knows, understands, and likes people, and he listens and pays attention. His networks are huge, varied, and intertwined. As the CEO of the Victor C. Neumann Foundation of Chicago, Carl calls on his long-time friends when he needs political support. He has street smarts and savvy. His sense of people, politics, and process has helped catapult his association from

The Flavor of Favors: Bittersweet

We need to make sure that we have earned the right to [ask] for a favor. Donna Epstein, Marin realtor and the consummate considerate networker, cautions that we shouldn't over-[tax] our contacts by asking for too many favors. History tells [us] that when Ben Franklin wanted to have a friendship with [some]one, he first loaned that person a book. He gave a favor [al]so that he could ask for one when the occasion arose. [We] want to ask people to assist us in ways that they may [com]fortably do so. To ask a person for something he or she [can]not deliver causes a strain.

When asking for favors, be appropriate. Have you earned [the] right to ask? "Favors are gifts to be appreciated and [retur]ned in kind and in spirit," offers Donna Epstein. Her dad [has] many sports connections, and a relative has access to [seats] in the entertainment world. She values them, and she [does]n't ask for favors. Because both of these men are gener[ous,] they derive joy in doing favors for friends and for charity. [The]y are important, not the tickets to whatever." A good [remi]nder.

The best networkers value, honor, and respect people for [who] *they are,* not for what they can do. Donna embodies the [art] of networking at its finest. She shares, refers, follows [thro]ugh, and is a matchmaker in the best sense of the term.

[R]eminders

- [P]olitics is merely a process. It is present in every phase of life.
- [W]e should not be fazed by politics, but accept it and increase [o]ur awareness of it.
- [R]eciprocity rules, because giving and taking are to be done on [b]alance.
- [M]anage your markers; know who you owe and who owes you, [a]nd whom you can ask.

a half-million-dollar base to a seven-million-dollar base. Who Carl LaMell *is* contributes to what he does, which is to assist persons with mental disabilities to function in society.

Hedging Our Bets

We all want to hedge our bets in the poker game of life. One way to do so is to listen to Big Jule. Our network will stop supporting us if we don't pay back. We need to know what chits are out there, who holds our markers (and for what), and whose markers are in our possession. Our positions in our networks and professions depend on it.

Savvy people know and understand that where people gather, politics permeates every group, in every phase of life: education, charity organizations, medicine, business, religion. It is not a sad commentary; it just *is.*

Savvy people waste not a moment whining or worrying about the presence of politics; instead they have the presence of mind to be mindful of it. Savvy people who are politically astute know the score. We all can name people who "don't know the score"; they just don't get it. They are, as a friend so aptly put it, "the clue-impaired."

Favor-itism

Brenda Besdansky, of Speakers World, received a call from a man who wanted to "pick her brain" about speakers' bureaus and marketing speakers. "We spent a lot of time on the phone where I was clearly giving my ideas, resources, and time. After several calls, I told him that my giving free advice didn't work for me and I wanted to explore with him some possible means of reciprocation. He quickly got off the phone. Several days later I received a letter from him stating that my 'request for reciprocation was a burden.' As if my giving him free consultations was fun for me!"

It is wise to recognize when a favor has been done for

us. It is prudent to know that we owe a favor in return. Recognizing that we owe a chit is as prudent as knowing we are owed. It is part of knowing the score. The network knows when we owe, and when we have or have not been paying up. Like Santa, we know who's been bad or good!

People express discomfort at recognizing that they have been given help or favors. We are undone by the thought of asking for help, let alone calling in old favors. The reality is that we *must* ask for the return of favors for several reasons: (1) It relieves people of the pressure and guilt of owing us; (2) it gives people an opportunity to give—which clears the slate so that they can continue to accept our favors, comfortably; (3) and we receive the help, advice, and contacts that we need.

Miss Fripp—Our Favor-ite

In addition, we may call in our markers to help others. That is precisely what my good friend Patricia Fripp, a top business motivator, did. The results were awesome.

In April of 1991 Patricia was asked to participate in a fund-raising competition. The enticement was that the top woman or man would appear on ten billboards in San Francisco. Patricia Fripp had wanted to be on billboards for fifteen years.

So Patricia Fripp drafted a letter and sent it to her colleagues, clients, cohorts, and cronies. She knew whose markers she held!

In her letter she asked people, "If I have ever done you a favor, listened to an audio of your speech, bought a wedding gift, recommended a client, given you a referral, given your organization a free speech, please assist me now. I am calling in my chits. For two reasons: (1) to raise the funds to support the Leukemia Society in their research, and (2) because I want to be the Hastings Woman of the Year."

The response was overwhelming. In six weeks, Patricia Fripp collected $30,000 (her closest competitor collected $16,000). Patricia was on the road giving presentations for the majority of those six weeks and not at home for more than four days. The night of the event she was in Indianapolis, but

---

fifteen of us were in San Francisco to cheer share her triumph.

"What is so amazing is that people who I h: send $25 sent huge amounts of money! I was and so touched by their generosity," confide

But those of us who know her have been her generosity, advice, energy, goodwill, ki good humor for years. She called in her mar for the Leukemia Society, and she continues

And, by the way, we all received a follow ing a copy of the billboard photo. Now the sl

---

A Mafia-li

Growing up in Chicago was an educa experience. I knew where the St. Valentine took place, and that there is a piper to important, what will happen if we don't pay. like Big Jule again. Trust me on this one. served me well in my three lives: urban urbane) schoolteacher, professional speaker I offer it to you for your consideration, success. While we may receive from our net to it solidifies our standing.

The Balancing Act—

Favors are tricky: They obligate the reci also has to be careful in how he or she gr: must give, or even create, an opportunity f

Some people are superb at getting make the giver feel fortunate to grant the understand this, most of us tend to move a reason. We walk highly wired tightropes, grace—and high wire—is deadly. We have receivers, and that's the beauty of balance

---

ask
ma
use
us
son
firs

con
can

the
retu
has
ever
doe
ous,
"Th
rem

who
spiri
thro

R

➤

➤

➤

➤

➤ Call in favors for yourself, for others or for charity to clear the slate.
➤ Pay back favors without being asked.
➤ Manage your markers. Homework:

List One—People Who Have Done Me Favors

1.
2.
3.
4.
5.

List Two—People for Whom I Have Done Favors

1.
2.
3.
4.
5.

This exercise is to assist you in being aware.

6

▶ ▶ ▶ ▶ ▶ ▶ ▶ ▶ ▶ ▶ ▶ ▶ ▶ ▶ ▶ ▶ ▶

Matchmaker, Matchmaker, Make Me a Match or... Leads, Referrals or Contacts

Yenta the Networker

In 1989 the silver anniversary tour of *Fiddler on the Roof* played in San Francisco. I expected Tevye's three daughters to sing an updated version: "Networker, networker, make me a match!" Wouldn't it be great to have "Yenta* the Networker," to fill all our business needs, goals and wishes?

"Oh, you need a florist? Have I got a florist for you! Doug Sharpe is fabulous!"

"A graphic designer? No problem! Sadie's son is such a talent!"

"Oh, you want a job as a financial analyst? This match will cost extra. Let me see, the Milken boy... he may know of a job in the industry. Excuse me, he is detained, making license plates, I hear. Let's take another look...."

By the way, in my vision, this Yenta the Networker resembles Bea Arthur, who was the original Yenta on Broadway. Don't be cranky or she'll call Shady Pines and reserve you a room!

*See Glossary.

In essence, the best of networkers are matchmakers because they:

1. Listen to your needs
2. Hear what you are and are not saying
3. Know many people, either directly or indirectly
4. Share their resources
5. Offer to make the match directly or allow you to use their names

Yenta did her good works for a finder's fee, which in some professions is expected. In others it's appropriate, although not required. You know your industry and the legal and ethical parameters. In chapter 7 we propose a list of potential acknowledgements in lieu of a finder's fee. Yenta the Networker gets as much satisfaction from making a match as Yenta the Matchmaker did.

Proof Positive

The respondents to a book survey, who "put people together successfully," enjoyed the results of making a match. Donna Epstein takes pride in having introduced her dear friend, a very successful entrepreneur desiring to expand her business, to a contact. The result: Donna's friend created an alliance with the contact that resulted in the successful sale of her business.

Chris Bigelow, Kansas City–based international consultant in the concession food industry, wrote, "All of my business is by word of mouth, and I assist others who do keep me apprised of their progress. I am always proud that I had a little to do with their success, which increases my stock as a good human resource source." Chris Bigelow is also one of the funniest people I've met; his humor is a magnet.

The survey respondents, who indicated that they were apprised of results when they assisted others, all felt good. Mortgage broker Bill Johnston has sometimes been surprised with the recognition he has received. "I often feel I am just doing my job. Buying a house is stressful enough, but going through the process of financing the loan is additional stress. So I try to be more calm, helpful, and generous with my praise. When people respond positively and appreciatively, I feel terrific! Whether the expression of gratitude is a note, a bottle of wine, or another referral, I feel great and am always willing to be of more assistance! I *always* follow up with my own note of thanks to my clients and often send them a gift to thank them for being my client."

Martin Swig, the pioneer of the "multi-franchising concept" in automobile dealerships, has always assisted people, but "I learned that you don't do things for the thanks; you do it because it helps someone else."

Risk of Referrals

Yes, there is always the risk that the "match" is not made in heaven. Perhaps the chef had an off night at your favorite restaurant, one you enthusiastically recommended to your best client; the movers were careless; the marketing professional who decided to market professional speakers did not know he was in the "meetings industry"; or the word processor did not like the words that had to be processed. There's that inexplicable thing called chemistry, as well as personality conflicts. Referrals and recommendations are always a risk. "To the risk-takers go the rewards," is the philosophy of David Smith, a professional speaker who is an adventurer and king of the risk-takers. David has kayaked the Nile and swum from Africa to Europe in a shark cage. He even tried to teach me to swim! Since he has taken risks to life and limb, referrals don't seem as risky.

Jonathan Ziegler, an investment analyst, took a risk that worked out to be a serendipitous reward. "A local business columnist, who had just moved to San Francisco, visited our offices. I thought of a great friend to fix him up with. When I called him to make the match, he said he was married and had three children. He must have appreciated my thoughtfulness though. He has reciprocated by often quoting me in his syndicated column."

Yenta the Headhunter

Executive recruiters and employment agencies exist to recruit, screen, and recommend qualified candidates for appropriate employment positions. For a predetermined fee, they provide a formal process of interviewing, résumé reviewing, testing, reference checking, and placement of the most appropriate, qualified candidate. Recruiters are networkers whose successful matches determine their business success.

I Heard It Through the Grapevine

Most of us have had a job that we heard about through a friend, acquaintance, or relative—whether it was baby-sitting for the Skov children, interning for the summer at LucasFilm's Skywalker Ranch, selling computer software to libraries, teaching in an experimental program for special children, or editing manuscripts for a publishing house.

We have told our buddies about openings that we hear of through the grapevine. The process is ancient. There are people who stand out because they manage the process with great aplomb. And there are those who stand out because they do not; they are "aplomb dumb." The following sections will give you guidelines for giving and getting leads and referrals.

Formal networking organizations have their own rules like Le Tip International. Leads clubs may differ from Le Tip, which may differ from other business alliance clubs. Before you join a formal lead-sharing group, read the literature, attend a meeting, observe and assess the process. Decide if that process works for you.

Humble Beginnings

Twelve years ago, attorney-mediator Esta Swig was writing wills as a public service. "A client recommended a couple who came to me for a fifty-dollar will. A while later the wife came to my office with her best friend's husband. Her best friend had been hit by a car and, to this day, is still in a nursing home. We settled the suit for $1.5 million! The victim is the mother of five children, who were little at the time. So I met with an officer of the trust department of Bank of America and arranged for him to manage the money as an investment so that the settlement would make money. The $65,000 per year interest income allows my client to have a private nurse in addition to placement in an excellent nursing facility. My other goal was to have the principal untouched so she could bequeath it to her children."

Esta Swig did more for her client than file suit; she has seen to it that this woman is cared for, as are her children. It was a lucrative case that all began from an unsolicited client referral for a fifty-dollar will and a subsequent, unexpected referral.

So let us not judge people based solely on our perceptions of a good referral, potential, well-connected lead, or who dresses well or lives in the right neighborhood. Some of the most lucrative leads come from surprising sources.

The Misjudge Mistake

This is a perfect place to reiterate that old adage we heard growing up: "Don't judge a book by its cover." If we do, we risk the error of *mis*judging.

Irv Spivak, a founder of the San Francisco Chamber of Commerce Business Alliance, reminds us, "Don't discount someone because they are starting a small business and may be a sole practitioner. You never know who that individual knows, to whom she is related, or with whom she is friends. It is wise to treat each person with respect."

We never know who will grow up and turn out well! The C students do, so be nice to them, especially if they are your children. They're the ones who'll support you in your old age.

Contacts in Context

Referrals are gifts that we are given, not a God-given right. How do you get referrals?

Some people have said that we should be straightforward, honest, and just ask for what we want. Be clear with yourself about what you want and need. But be careful about asking for ideas and referrals from someone with whom you have no established communication, rapport, or relationship. It may be better if you let your needs be known, rather than ask directly. That allows the other person time to think without being on the spot.

Sherris Goodwin, owner of the Hospitality Institute, is one of the most generous people I know. Over dinner we were discussing some of the societal changes we had observed in our decade-long friendship, and the lack of manners and/or savvy that seems to be prevalent in business. "The other night a young woman ["Rhonda"] attended our local NAWBO [National Association of Women Business Owners] meeting, and heard me talk about my work, the institute and my business trip to Russia. I had barely exchanged words with her when she said, 'I'd love to have lunch with you and get your contacts.'" Oy vay!*

I was stunned. Have decorum and delicacy disappeared? But Sherris is generous and patient and offered to give this person "the names of four contacts with the stipulation that she call me in three months with a follow-up report." Sherris said she will give Rhonda more information and leads, if she hears from her. "It's my experience that ninety percent of

*See Glossary.

these people do not follow-up with leads they are given. That is why I stopped making the pre-lead call to warm up the contact. When Rhonda has proven her mettle, then I'll assist her further," explains Sherris.

I asked her why she thought this bright woman could be so lacking in savvy as to assume that she deserved Sherris's leads. "Somewhere these young (and dumb) people, who may have book smarts, heard that networking meant they get to have everyone's contacts." We all know people like that, even those who are old and dumb and presumptuous.

Networking is not an entitlement program; it is an enrichment program.

Hard and Smart Work... Works

Most of the people I surveyed are referred by clients because their work is superb. Rich Gold explained that, as a strategic planning and management consultant, his clients approach him. "For me to advertise or solicit business would be inefficient and ineffective. Clients need to have confidence that I can help solve their problems and create opportunities. If I have to approach them, I must 'need' the business and that doesn't build client confidence. However, if they approach me because of a referral, their comfort zone is larger."

Dan Donovan does not ask his clients for referrals, but he gets most of his new clients through his present ones, many of whom are now friends. "I am very careful to listen and to ask questions so that I can meet the needs of each client, especially their risk-aversion level. While I always tangibly acknowledge each referral, I never reveal any information beyond that the friend is now a client."

A writer I met at a business event told me that he gets most of his business through referrals. I gave him the name of someone who could use his services and made it clear we were pals. In a subsequent conversation, he made some negative comments about my friend in relation to the time he invested in their exploratory conversation: "My time is too valuable to be wasted by people who aren't ready to commit to hiring me." Yet this man thought nothing of wasting my time. And he wanted more leads from me that I had clearly qualified as solid, potential clients who could immediately hire him. His attitude was so self-indulgent and his behavior so lacking in savvy that I decided I would not refer any more clients to him. It would be a "match made in hell."

Family Ties

Extended networks are like extended family. Bill Gillis, president of INFO Enterprises, and I met at a business networking event almost a decade ago. We both believe in extended networks. "The most striking example of this method of networking involves my now college-aged son," Gillis says. "Having recently moved to a new town, leaving old friends, and contending with me as a demanding parent—he was down in the dumps and not performing up to his capabilities in school. One evening he was lamenting that he would be unable to complete an assignment because it required some personal interaction with the person who was the subject of the paper. After discussing prospective subjects, it was clear that he wanted to use Andrew Young, then Atlanta mayor, as his subject.

"After a bit of reflection, I recalled that an acquaintance of long standing was both Atlanta-based and was active in the Greater Atlanta Chamber of Commerce. I placed a call to her, explained the situation, and asked for any suggestions she might have on contacting Mayor Young. She suggested that she could contact the mayor and have him send an autographed picture to my son, fulfilling the 'personal contact' requirement of the paper. When I further explained my son's 'blue funk,' she indicated that she'd ask Mayor Young to send along a few words of encouragement. In just a few days the photo bearing words of encouragement arrived. The paper received an A and my son's outlook brightened immeasurably. The true power of networking! The joy was that my network helped my son...and I could see the impact."

"During a business trip," shared Chuck Jones, "I was having dinner with my uncle and we were catching up on things. He was telling me about his business plans and I asked him who was going to do the expansion for the company. When he said that he didn't know, I asked, 'What about me?' After some discussions and consulting work for the company, my uncle hired me. I had the background and experience. So now I am vice president of sales at TiltRac Corporation. Family is part of our networks."

A Network Nudge*

Another speaker, Barbie the Bully, called me several years ago after I gave a presentation that was highly promoted. "Susan, I want to speak for that group. Could I have your contact's name and number?" This was a woman I hardly knew and we had barely exchanged words; she was in no position to ask. Such nerve! When I gently stammered that this was not a good idea, she persisted in virtually demanding the information. I was taken aback, felt bullied, and capitulated. Was I ever angry at myself for being such a pushover!

There is a better way to encourage people to give us leads and contacts and to avoid putting them on the spot. People who are backed into corners often come out fighting.

"Susan, I read that you spoke to the Wheeler Dealers Association. That's a group I would really like to address. If you think there is a fit, I'd love the name and number of the meeting planner for a future conference."

Yes, this is a soft sell; Barbie the Bully could be Barbie the Better-Behaved. Yet she taught me a special lesson. Just because someone else wants a lead, a donation, a lunch appointment, doesn't mean I am obligated to say yes. Neither are you.

*See Glossary.

When Barbie the Bully called the lead, she misused my name, implying I was endorsing her with my referral. But life has an amusing way of providing interesting opportunities. When the conference planner called to talk with me about Barbie, I made it clear that I merely complied with Barbie's request to give her the name and number, and that I could not recommend Barbie, as I had never heard her give a speech. That's the truth...which can come back to haunt the untruthful.

Meeting Your Match—Inform-Ally

Much of matchmaking (networking) happens informally, which, if we take another look, is *inform-ally:* We inform an ally about a job, a local service, or a new product. Linda Mantel, vice president of the Tom Peters Group/Learning Systems (TPG/LS), did just that. "I gave myself a sabbatical to spend some time deciding what my life's work would be. I told everyone I knew about the position that I was seeking, including Marcia Teitelbaum, who used to work with me at Shaklee and has been a friend for years [our mutual friend and introducer]. Marcia told me of a position at a small training company, for which I then interviewed. It wasn't what I wanted, and the fellow gave me the name of someone who knew of another open position. I called and learned of the opening at TPG."

My Friend → Job Interview → Interviewer's Contact → TPG/LS

Mantel adds, "My advice is to be willing to call everyone you know and let them know."

Don't Forget Old Friends

The world works in wonderful ways. Patti Breitman, Marin-based literary agent, got her first job in publishing through Helaine Katz, an old friend from camp days. "I was a secretary for a publishing house in New York, working for a marketing manager with whom I stayed in touch over the years. He's now the vice president and publisher at Harper-Collins and he just bought one of my client's books."

Joe Griffith, a Dallas-based author and speaker, says that one of his friends from first grade is the chairman of a Fortune 500 company, a contact that has led to many opportunities.

Susan Witkin, a reporter and news anchor for KGO radio in San Francisco, had her career path altered because her friend from Hebrew school bumped into her mother and asked about Susan. "When my mom said I was going to school in Durango, he was thrilled. He worked at a radio station that was covering a murder trial and the venue was changed to Durango. He arranged for me to cover the trial. I called United Press International and a big Denver television station, figuring they'd be interested, too, and they were. The rest is history."

People from our pasts may have impact on our personal and professional lives because we have stayed in touch.

RoAne's Rules for Matchmaking

Referrals can happen on the golf course, in the health club, at the barbershop, at the nonprofit agency's board meeting, in the bleachers at Wrigley Field, or at a bridal shower. Networking is now about the exchange of ideas, information, and leads…a rare recipe.

We need to:

1. Let people know what we are looking for
2. Do it in a way that allows them to respond comfortably
3. Keep our matchmakers apprised of the progress and outcome of their efforts
4. Acknowledge appropriately and in a timely fashion
5. Reciprocate whenever possible

Maybe in the golden anniversary revival of *Fiddler,* they will sing "Networker, networker, cast out your net...match me a match, which I won't forget...."

And we must never forget to acknowledge those networkers who have made referrals and matches for us.

Reminders

➤ Referrals are made through:
  • Formal lead-generating organizations which have their own rules
  • Semiformal professional associations and trade shows
  • Informally—as a matter of due course
➤ Networking is matchmaking, listening for a need, and arranging for a crony, colleague or client to fill it.
➤ A job done well is the best advertisement.
➤ No matter how many organizations we join, direct-mail pieces we send, cold calls we place—we must have an excellent personal as well as professional reputation.
➤ Recommendations should be tracked, acknowledged, and followed with progress reports.
➤ Extended networks are an important resource.
➤ People enjoy assisting others in their endeavors.
➤ The people who stand out either do so because of their gracious manner or lack thereof.
➤ The networking nuisance who demands leads is misled.
➤ Don't forget old friends; they are more than part of your network, they are part of your history.
➤ **Networking is an enrichment program, not an entitlement program.**

7

▶▶▶▶▶▶▶▶▶▶▶▶▶▶▶▶

Thanks for the Memories

"Let us give thanks," is the comment that precedes a prayer and has direct application to us. Without giving thanks, we will not "have a prayer" in the process known as networking.

Acknowledgement is the cornerstone of alliance building and common courtesy. There is just no way to get around it, nor should we even try. There is truly magic in doing so. We should not wait until the fourth Thursday of November to give thanks.

The Magic Words

Remember being taught the magic words "please" and "thank you"? Hopefully, you teach them diligently to your children. Generations of parents have spent energy and time teaching their offspring the "magic words." "Oh, Joey, look at the wonderful book Grandma bought you! What do you say?" A scene from *Look Who's Talking* may flash in your head and you may hear Bruce Willis's voice say, "Jeez, a book. I can't even read. Why couldn't Grandma bring me a toy, one that I can break in five minutes or less!"

But the real answer is "thank you." The result: Grandma

is in seventh heaven with her polite genius and, of course, rarely appears without some tchotchkes* for Joey.

How does this scene play in our adult lives? With great relevance. It's simple. Most people appreciate being appreciated. I still have thank-you notes from Steven (ten) and Charles (twelve) Cherezian for Christmas gifts, donations to their spellathons, and books I sent for their research projects. They learned to express appreciation from their parents, my friends, Sylvia and the late Gregg Cherezian, who took the time to impart the value and format of the thank-you note.

It's never too late to learn. If this were not the case, Abby and Ann, the Dispensing Twins of Daily Advice, would have less mail. Miss Manners is also often queried by her readers on the same issues. If most of us teach our children to say "Please" and "Thank you," they must be valuable words worth saying ourselves.

Millions of dollars are spent annually to train managers and supervisors in techniques that will increase productivity. Secretaries are trained in phone techniques that reflect good practices. Are we overlooking a practical technique—acknowledgement? Most people in the work force feel better and perform better when their efforts are acknowledged.

The opposite of appreciating the contributions of co-workers, subordinates, and friends is ignoring them. Being taken for granted is a negative feeling that can make a person feel used. That is unproductive.

Countless columns on business behavior deal with customer, client, employee, boss, and secretary appreciation. Why? Because it is sorely lacking. Why? The reasons are better left to the sociologists, psychologists, and pollsters. I prefer to propose some remedies: A Back to Basics Blueprint.

Susan's Socratic Reasoning

My basic premise is that no one owes us a lead, lunch, referral, energy, time, advice, or favor of any type. Therefore, if any of these are bestowed on us, we must acknowledge—appropriately and in a timely fashion. This is not up for

*See Glossary.

discussion; it just is. In *Leadership Is an Art,* Max De Pree states that the "responsibility of a leader is to say thank you."[21]

The Problem—in Three Parts

There is a problem and it's a three-parter:

1. Some people do not value that which is given to them or shared with them.
2. Others do not verbalize their appreciation.
3. Still others do not demonstrate it.

Gift Gaffe

Many people do know that a gift requires a thank-you note. To my chagrin, too many people do not. A gift is something you can eat, drink, read, wear, smell, utilize in home or office, or deposit in the bank.

A reader wrote Miss Manners several years ago to complain that she was a "busy professional who simply did not have the time to write notes for her wedding gifts." Miss Manners, as one would expect, showed her no mercy. "If you do not have the time to acknowledge the generosity of the guests who cele- brated your wedding, then you do not have the time to use those gifts, nor deposit the monetary ones. Because you lack the time to enjoy them, you must then *return them all.*"[22]

I would offer the suggestion of one lecture participant: "Where does it say that writing thank-you notes is the bride's job? It is the couple's responsibility, a great opportunity to share fifty-fifty." Maybe that's why they say people are "groomed" for positions.

Timely Tips

The massive corporate layoffs, mergers and acquisitions, and recession of the early 1990s have impacted careers. People are falling off the top of the corporate ladder; the trickle-down effect has been a stunning blow. The ability to

value, verbalize, and demonstrate appreciation will differenti-
ate you in a competitive marketplace...in a positive way.
Sources of support expand rather than contract. Acknowledging reflects breeding...appreciation breeds content.

Do you express appreciation to bosses, coworkers, friends,
and family? Do you give verbal attribution to those who have
had a positive impact on your career? Or do such activities
"take too much time"?

- A meal, beverage, or party hosted, paid for, or prepared by
  someone else merits a thank-you. And for the legions of
  people who prepare and serve meals for spouses, offspring,
  parents, and friends, a simple "Thank you" might be music
  to their ears. People are aware of those times when they
  have made a special effort to do a favor and it's not
  acknowledged or appreciated.
- A favor is defined as a kindness or gift. Office or workplace
  favors might include: special research for a project, a copy
  of a magazine article of interest, an immediate typing of a
  report, support for an extension of a project deadline.
- Work completed thoroughly, prior to deadline, creatively
  and cost-effectively, is special.
- Contacts and referrals that you have been given for possible
  clients, informational interviews, job leads, and organizations are valuable.
- Time, given as a kindness, takes many forms: a phone
  conversation where you receive or request advice or information, an office visit to a coworker when you are stuck on
  a problem, or a letter of commendation or recommendation
  that takes time to draft, type, and mail.

If time is the commodity you wish you had more of, how
can you receive time from others and not have the time to
indicate appreciation? People have said that they think about
doing something but think they don't have time, are not good
at that sort of thing, are not organized—hogwash! This is a
cop-out, and if your goal is to expand your resources and
contact base, that attitude will be counterproductive. We all
have the same number of hours in our day. The basic truth is

that we have the time and money for our priorities. Most of the survey respondents indicated that they always send gifts to clients and to the person who referred a client. They appreciate the business and let that be known.

Some questions you may consider:

- Do you take time to drop into an office to interrupt a colleague so you can get help? If so, then you have the time to acknowledge that help.
- Do you have time to convince the boss's secretary to schedule you for a brief meeting? Then you have time to demonstrate your appreciation.
- Do you have time to call a crony when you want the lowdown on a mutual acquaintance in your industry? Then you have time to say "Thanks!"

Vast sums of money are spent teaching people how to build rapport and business relationships. My buddy Jim Cathcart, speaker and author, shares essential relationship strategies, the basis of which is to take the time necessary to establish rapport.

Janice Peters and Barbara Vogel of Access Speakers Bureau in Little Rock are two people who take the time. "This is just the way we like to run our business, knowing our clients. It feels good to pick up the phone knowing we are going to call a speaker or meeting planner who is a friend. The time we have taken for those friendships is well worth it."

Time Is of the Essence

If you have time to receive help, favors, gifts, advice, you would be wise to make time to give acknowledgement. If not, your sources of support could dry up. As well they should! There is a written code of behavior—etiquette—and there is an unwritten code. And we are judged by our adherence to both. It therefore behooves us to learn and practice both codes. It is well worth the time and career to do so.

What can happen if you don't show appreciation or acknowledgement or give thanks? Plenty or nothing. It depends on your vantage point…or disadvantage point. Your resources will dry up, plain and simple.

Lead Loser

Jeff Slutsky, a talented speaker, "Streetfighter," and author of *How to Get Clients,* was asked by a client to design a full-day conference on marketing. He took the request seriously and booked three other presenters to give portions of the program. One gent, a marketing professor at a Big Ten university, was booked by Jeff for his client at the professor's fee of $5,000. "He gave a good presentation," said Jeff, "and he earned $5,000." Sounds like a good enough reason for the professor to be "appreciative." Maybe he was, but no one knows, especially not Jeff. "I never heard from him, not a call nor note nor any visible token of acknowledgement." A "thank-you for recommending me to give a one-and-a-half-hour presentation for $5,000" was unquestionably in order. The professor needs to go back to school—charm school—where etiquette, manners, and a class or two in common courtesy are taught.

Surely there is no law enforcing violations of appreciation, though I wish it were so ("Manners Maids" on their scooters, ticketing the thoughtless). But there is a higher law, unenforceable in the courts—and that higher law affects "hire" law.

Three months later, the client called Jeff and asked him to pull together the same program for a different regional office. Having received no acknowledgement and several of his calls left unreturned, Jeff offered the regional office a different speaker. The professor lost $5,000 and there are five more regional conferences that he will not address, a total income loss of $30,000. Given Jeff's position and history of recommending speakers, amortized over a ten-year period, the professor could lose $100,000 in speaking fees. No thank-you, no referrals. That's the rule. Once burned, twice shy.

Each person reading this book has similar tales to share of people who breach basic acts of common courtesy and common sense. A similar situation happened to a Silicon Valley stockbroker. Breach of common courtesy is an understated description of her referral rip-off. "We had some remodeling to do on our home and hired a local design architect who did a good job. I referred several clients to her; one hired her to do a job worth about $10,000. Months went by, not a note nor a word of appreciation for a 'healthy' referral. Due to circumstances one month, we were five days late with our payment. Within two days, a formal letter and invoice with interest arrived. We were furious." The stockbroker did not give silent approval to this exhibition of Bad Business/ Bad Behavior. They sent the payment and late charge with a letter. In this letter, she made it clear that the ignored referral showed incredibly bad manners and bad business sense. Not only would they "no longer refer business to the architect, they would *actively discourage* any of their friends and associates." Ultimate cost—incalculable.

The architect had every right to send a late-payment notice and charge a late fee; but this is someone who didn't notice that her former client's referral had increased her coffers by $10,000.

Perhaps some of you are thinking: "This is beyond basic, it is remedial." So be it. If business people (who ought to know better) were responding appropriately, the Three R's— RoAne's Remedial Reminders—would be unnecessary. The bottom line is that people appreciate being appreciated. Use those magic words . . . *please* and *thank you*!

The Magic of Threes

Step One: Do you value people and their contributions to you? Then Steps Two and Three will be easy. The person who does not value others is stuck and cannot proceed to Step Two.

Step Two: Verbalize your acknowledgement:
"*Thanks* for the [report, idea, lunch, time]."
"I *appreciate* the time you took to give me some job search ideas."

Truly, the *italicized* words indicate the emphasis of your comments. As Grandma said, IT IS NOT JUST WHAT YOU SAY, BUT *HOW* YOU SAY IT. That rings true.

Step Three: Demonstrating your appreciation:

A sincere note of thanks is the basic proof of appreciation, not a sales tool invented by a trainer. By virtue of the term, a thank-you *note* is *not* a letter. It certainly is not typed or word-processed no matter how efficient those options might be. A thank-you note is handwritten on paper of good stock. It is not a fax. It is not a "rote note," but one that expresses *sincere* appreciation. A former teacher colleague was (and is) the world-class "rote note" sender: glowing, flowing words of thanks handwritten on fine paper. The notes did not ring true. Perfunctory, lacking heart, soul, sincerity, and to be avoided at all costs.

Ah, you are too busy to take two minutes to write two sentences. Tsk, tsk. If that is your reaction, please reread this chapter. The test is every day...in every phase of life.

Giving Thanks

The form of the expression of appreciation must be commensurate with the contribution, and there are times when a thank-you note is not enough. Some of these times:

• A referral to a job that you get
• A lead to a client that turns into dollars
• A favor that saves you valuable time and money

Let's go back to Jeff Slutsky and the professor who earned $5,000 as a result of Jeff's recommendation. In some professions, a referral fee is inappropriate and even illegal. In the speaking profession, where bureaus that book speakers receive twenty-five to thirty percent of the fee, a ten percent thank-you is not inappropriate. Of course, that depends on your relationship with the person who referred you, and the agreements you have about shared leads.

If paying a referral fee felt awkward, there are other ways in which Mr. Not-So-Savvy Professor could have said "Thanks." Some ideas:

• Flowers or balloons
• Food, wine, cookies, candy assortments (many entrepreneurs and shops provide this service)
• Magazine gift subscriptions
• Gifts (most major department stores have executive shoppers to help you select)
• Tickets to sports or cultural events (baseball, ballet or theater)
• Lunch or dinner (restaurants have gift certificates)
• Or even a book!

How might you know what is appropriate? Well! If you take the time to talk and listen to people and jot a note to help you remember, the task is easy.

An Honorable Thank-you

One very special gift that continues to give is a donation to a charity in honor of the person to be thanked. Most charities will send a note to the honoree. National organizations like the March of Dimes and the Leukemia Society, as well as local literacy, AIDS, and heart associations, need our assistance. Because of the recent death of two friends, I support organizations doing breast cancer research. By supporting charities important to the recipient, your gratitude is expressed in a most meaningful manner.

As I write this, I glance up and see a magnificent hill full of various types of trees. Even before the current reforestation movement, trees were very important to me. They are a source of peace, serenity, and great beauty. As children we collected money for the Jewish National Fund to plant trees in Israel. My cohorts and I always felt we made a contribution to the blooming of the desert. (Yes, every Borscht Belt comic tells the story that there is only one forest in Israel, and the nameplates are switched for the current visiting donor.)

As an adult, I buy trees in honor of clients, colleagues, and friends. I have had one planted in memory of a friend's loved one, even one in honor of a colleague who received an award.

Do people appreciate these gifts? Do you? Of course! They have meaning; they are trees of life.

And because we value the contributions of others, acknowledgements that are meaningful and sincerely meant... are magic. The ability to make these acknowledgements helps us maintain and expand our sources and resources while we acknowledge others.

Quiz of Note

Which of these notes would you prefer to receive?

Sample Personal Thank-you Notes:

Don't:

> *Dear Joan and John,*
>
> *Thank you for the lovely wedding gift. It will be put to good use in our new home.*
>
> > *Sincerely,*
> >
> > *Mary and Marvin*

Do:

> *Dear Joan and John,*
>
> *Thank you so much for sharing our wedding celebration. We really appreciate the toaster oven; it will be put to good use, as we both love our daily toasted bagels. The toaster's timer will end our burnt bagel problem!*
> *Thanks again.*
>
> > *Cordially,*
> >
> > *Mary and Marvin*

Sample Professional Thank-you Notes:

Don't:

> Dear Bob,
>
> *Thank you for meeting with me. I found your comments to be helpful.*
>
> > *Cordially,*
> >
> > *Susan RoAne*

Passable, but the focus is on the writer, not the recipient.

Do:

> Dear Bob,
>
> *I really appreciate the time you took from your busy day to talk with me. You gave me much food for thought, a smorgasbord of ideas for me to ponder. You certainly expanded my thinking and I am grateful.*
> *Thank you again. I look forward to returning your support.*
>
> > *Cordially,*
> >
> > *Susan RoAne*

More expressive; focuses on the reader; more energy.

Sending the appropriate note that expresses thanks speaks volumes. It is always appreciated by anyone who has given a gift or hosted a meal.

Reminders

➤ Remember these magic words... *please* and *thank you*.

➤ Acknowledge the following:
- Gifts
- Time
- Favors
- Meals
- Ideas
- Leads

➤ Value contributions.

➤ Verbalize your appreciation:
- Face-to-face
- Phone
- Fax
- Answering machine

➤ Demonstrate gratitude... appropriately:
- Thank-you notes (handwritten)
- Flowers
- Food
- Gifts
- Donations

8

▷ ▷ ▷ ▷ ▷ ▷ ▷ ▷ ▷ ▷ ▷ ▷ ▷ ▷ ▷ ▷ ▷ ▷

Lunch Pails by Comparison or Let's "Do" Lunch and Business

Some business phrases sound like fingernails on a chalkboard. One is "I have to *take* a meeting." Really, where are you taking it—out of state? Another is "Let's do lunch." Why *do,* not *have*? Even more irritating is that some people use "Let's do lunch" as a conversation closer. To do that, we should say, "Good talking to you…take care." Or "Goodbye."

Back to lunch. There will always be the "business lunch." It's an opportunity to meet a potential client, colleague, associate or coworker "off campus." We get to break bread, share information, and have conversations that don't revolve around or take place in the office. And, hopefully, are not interrupted except by the server.

PDA—Public Displays of Affectation

With today's technology and ETSI (Escalating Toys of Self-Importance), the uninterrupted business lunch is not always the case.

Have you ever dined at restaurants where personal portable phones rang, and people talked to those at their table as well as to the caller? One morning I was having a business breakfast interview with a local newspaper reporter when I heard a patron speaking very loudly. He had a bad connection on his portable phone and regressed to long-distance phone techniques...shouting to enhance the connection! Of course, this man's business was very important...to him! But PDA (Public Displays of Affectation) are, at best, questionable—the word *rude* comes to mind.

Phone conversations during lunch are power plays that make an impression, and not necessarily a good one. It's an excellent method for treating your host, guest, or companions as second best.

However, there are exceptions: the heart surgeon who learns that a donor heart is now available for a transplant...a life-and-death matter.

Who Is Host?

The person who extends the invitation is the host, unless it is clear that the meal is "Dutch treat," which is often the case among coworkers and colleagues. The host is the person who will be "picking the brain" of the guest. If you use lunch as an opportunity for obtaining consultation or advice or for brainstorming, you pay. It doesn't matter who earns more; what counts is that the person who shares his/her time and information is the guest. *RULE:* He or she who PICKS brain PICKS up check.

The host is also the person in control of the location, agenda, and conversation. In the business world, "picking up the tab" is the power position. Some people exercise this right with such great warmth, charm, and panache that the guest is made to feel comfortable. With others, the power plays exceed the panache, and the guest would be more comfortable dining in the Reptile House at the local zoo with snakes of a different order.

Mega Meals and Deals

Some hosts control the conversation by asking questions so that the guest does all the talking/revealing, and the host contributes little to the communication. To some, it appears that the host is an interested listener. To others, that's manipulative and off-putting.

A business lunch has an implicit social aspect, or the meeting would take place in an office. The restaurant or lunch club provides an opportunity for common ground and social conversation. For example:

Questions:

"Have you been here before?"
"How is the food?"
"What would you recommend?"
"May I borrow your reading glasses to see the menu?"

Observations:

"The decor is tasteful."
"The view of the bay is magnificent!" (I live in San Francisco.)
"There seems to be ample street parking." (Purely wishful thinking in San Francisco.)
"The food is delicious, such unique combinations…mussels and kumquats."

Self-Disclosure:

"I always like to try new undiscovered restaurants where the food is ample."
"I prefer to stay with trusted, reliable restaurants I know."
"It took me thirty minutes to get a cab to get here in this rain!" (New York)

Since the beginning of time, food has been more talked about than eaten. Remember the first bite of the apple? Now we discuss cholesterol, calories, grams, presentation, flavor. All "food for thought" and conversation.

Power and control lunches have their place in the corporate wheelings and dealings that define and refine major business negotiations. But the business lunch designed to expand our circle of contacts is not a "P&C" meal.

Keeping Tabs

Sherris Goodwin, owner of the Hospitality Institute, remembers the period of her life when she owned the Fay Mansion Inn, a bed-and-breakfast in San Francisco, and many other properties. "That was a time when picking up a $2,000 tab for dinner and drinks was routine. My then associates and friends expected I'd always pay and, frankly, *so did I!*

"I'll never forget the morning I was having breakfast with a new business associate and friend who, though struggling in her new business, picked up the tab. I was so surprised. Nobody had done that in years. It was a generous, thoughtful gesture which made me realize that, while to the other 'friends' I was a meal ticket, to her I was a person. And we are now the best of friends."

My buddy Noah Griffin, a San Francisco talk-show host and syndicated columnist, tells this story of an acquaintance. "He had some questions he wanted to ask and we set a lunch date. He asked his questions and I did my best to answer them, coming up with ideas for him. When the check was brought to the table, he didn't budge. I ended up paying for lunch. He didn't even offer to split it. This man has a Ph.D., but his education is sorely lacking and it will surely sabotage him in a business setting. It already has." Each of you has a story or two like this. Feeling used is a horrible feeling. What can we do?

An Ounce of Prevention

One possibility is to say something when there is an expressed interest in the information you may share: "I'd be delighted to let you buy my time and my lunch! When and where would you like to take me?"

Some people will even say, "I'd like to get together to pick your brain." The picture that comes to mind is often disconcerting...they pick out the good parts, and I'll be without. "Oh! You want a consultation! I'd be pleased. Since we know there's no such thing as a free lunch, where would you like to take me?"

Sound gutsy? Feel uncomfortable? Any more uncomfortable than getting stuck with a tab?

Another issue around business lunch brainstorming is *time*.

Win-Win Lunch

I am open to spending ten to fifteen minutes on the phone with a prospective speaker, career changer, or author who has been given my name by someone in my network. It sure beats three hours for lunch, and there's a nice touch that I learned from a local stockbroker. I'll ask, "Have my leads and ideas been helpful?" (The answer is yes.) "Is it worth a lunch?" "Sure, I'll take you to lunch." "Thanks, I don't need the calories, but here's an alternative. Send me a check made out to St. Anthony's Dining Room for what the lunch would have cost. Let's take the ideas I shared and feed some hungry people." "That's a great idea!" is always the response.

It is a win-win. Give ten to fifteen minutes of support ideas and leads. The caller benefits, we both help feed the hungry, and we both feel really good!

The Host's Job

Hosts see to the comfort of their guests. They select a restaurant, call for a reservation, find out if the guest has special dietary needs, and arrange to leave a credit card with the manager so that there are no financial dealings at the table. Private clubs have this advantage. Most of the seasoned corporate executives are well versed in the formalities and amenities of hosting meals, meetings, and parties, or they would not be executives and leaders.

Some reminders: Guests are seated with their backs to the banquette; hosts face them. Hosts may give the meal order for everyone but may not choose the meals unless asked to do so. Hosts check with the guests to see if they would like more wine, dessert, etc. Remember, most aware guests do observe the leader.

Impeccable manners are an asset. Letitia Baldridge, Miss Manners, and a myriad of manners mavens serve up the rules. *Corporate Protocol,* by Valerie Grant-Sokolosky, serves up a concise manners menu and Tips on Tipping.

If the purpose of the meal is celebratory, calling ahead to arrange the surprise champagne or chocolate decadence mousse torte is a nice touch. Most restaurant personnel will cooperate.

Birthday Bash—Bashed

And the exceptions. My dear friend celebrated her first birthday as a mom. Dad baby-sat while I took her to the theater and to a lovely, posh, four-star restaurant. It was abundantly clear that I was hosting Terri Skov's birthday dinner. You can imagine my chagrin when the birthday cake was brought to the table while I was in the ladies' room. The server didn't see I was gone? At the end of dinner, the same "rocket scientist" placed the check at Terri's left arm—totally out of my reach. It was a 7.4 on the Richter scale of bad form as I prevailed upon my guest to hand me the check. I wrote a note on the check about both infractions, knowing the manager sees them when "cashing out." Most restaurateurs know they are not only in the food business, they're also in the service business. The service that night was "A Nightmare on Post Street."

Terri Skov is like a daughter to me. It would have been far

more embarrassing had this happened when I was hosting a client. It would have provided fuel for a conversation on the decline of service in America and some funny one-liners and vignettes. These are the moments that are mitigated by having a good sense of humor, easing the tension of any faux pas.

The Flip(pant) Side

We should be sure that we are being as gracious, congenial, and as clear as possible with restaurant personnel. At an elegant birthday lunch, friend and former teaching colleague Sylvia Cherezian and I observed a man hosting four women. The charm oozed in conversation with his four female associates, and the P&C (power and control) were visible and audible. But the tone he used with the server was patronizing, at best.

"How people treat service people is a very important reflection of character," observed Syl, who reminded me that we both had good relationships with the school secretary, custodians, and paraprofessionals. How we treat restaurant personnel is observed by our lunch companions and remembered. Let's make positive memories.

The Bagel Brouhaha

I don't cook very much. So I eat out often, where I do much of my writing. Sustenance for this chapter was provided at the Half-Day Cafe in Marin County. And so was this tale of mistreatment by a customer as related to me by the hostess, Lucille.

"This morning a customer came in and ordered coffee and a bagel with cream cheese, no butter. When he received the check, he screamed at me about the charge for cream cheese, which he substituted for butter. I explained that bagels are not on the menu as a single item, that we were trying to accommodate him, and that often cream cheese is an extra charge at most restaurants. He was rude and yelling unnecessarily and then stormed out saying, 'I'll never come back here again!' The sad thing is that, if he had been pleasant, I would have dropped the charge. All of this energy was expended over a $3.05 bill. What a waste!"

Good News for Guys in the Nineties

For many years women were the guests of the men in whose company they partook of meals, even those rare business meals, since few women were in the workplace. That has changed. Several of the men I interviewed admitted that "it felt awkward the first few times" they were the guests. How discreetly the bill was handled added to their comfort. They now "love being taken to lunch."

Maybe it's another opportunity for one-up*man*ship.... "How many women took you to lunch this month?" "Heh, heh, heh, I had five meals with women who picked up the tab." Again, the client is the guest, as is the information/lead/advice giver. The recipient (male or female) is the host.

The Guest List... of Do's and Don'ts

The list of appropriate guest behaviors is long. Guests are mindful that a hosted lunch may not be the time to order your two favorite dishes, caviar and lobster, unless the host recommends them and orders some. "What do you recommend?" is a question that gives your host the opportunity to provide some guidelines. Keep in mind, expense accounts are less generous these days.

Being a gracious guest includes being a good listener, as well as being conversant. We all must bring something to the Banquet of Banter. Your host will provide the guidelines of the lunch. If he does not indulge in an alcoholic beverage, you may want to follow suit.

When to Switch

When to segue from social conversation to the business at hand is as important as how to do so. The best time to discuss business is after the meal has been served and plates have been cleared. Lunch is about building communication and rapport and getting to know each other, and is less about eating (which we still should *not* do simultaneously...nor with our elbows on the table).

If every manager and potential executive really knew manners, corporate America would not have to hire experts to train their M.B.A.'s, CPAs, LL.B's, etc., in the rules of etiquette. And it's a growing industry; the more's the pity!

As It Is Written...

The guest should *always* send a thank-you note to the host, who, at the very least, provided sustenance. And if the host was provided sustenance in the form of leads, consultation, advice, feedback or ideas, a gift of acknowledgement is also appropriate. Remember, the gift of time is precious.

In building an ongoing business relationship, a handwritten note is personal and memorable. It indicates that you (not your secretary) took precious time to take pen in hand. Remember the impression made by the last handwritten note you received? I still have those I've received from Tom Peters, author of *In Search of Excellence* and *Thriving on Chaos.*

Today is the best time to start being a good guest...to write notes of thanks. And to teach your children the value, reasons, and format to do the same.

How to Avoid a "Splitting" Headache

There is not much that intimidates me: not an audience of one thousand, not a roomful of strangers, not a fear of flying! But three things do cause me *great* discomfort:

1. Turkeys (the birds, not people) and cooking them
2. People who *wash* silk, while the rest of us pay $6.95 to clean it!

3. The Great Divide. If the idea of involuntarily underwriting someone's caviar, lobster, and Dom Perignon when you are not the D.H. (designated host) annoys you, too, read on.

I have always accepted and encouraged the easier equal division of the dinner bill. The logic is that a few dollars are not important enough to waste time and energy dividing proportionately. I had an eight-month absence from social business restaurant dining to write my first book and to cure a case of vocal cord strain. Upon my return from my reclusiveness, I experienced four incidents in one month that made me feel ripped off when splitting tabs. In each incident I paid at least two and one half times my individual meal cost (including tax and tip).

Avoid Cheap-Skating on Thin Ice

Why did I stay quiet? I didn't want to appear cheap, nor to be perceived as ungracious. Yes, my fault, my problem. The real question is: Am I the only person in the world who suffers from the Dutch Treat Dilemma?

In hopes that I was not the only patsy, I decided to do an informal survey. So I called people and posed the situation to them. The results corroborated my discomfort *and* educated me. People were kind enough to be candid.

George McCabe, general manager of Ottawa Congress Center in Canada, agreed: "It's not worth the hassle for four or five dollars to spend the time and energy figuring out who ate and drank what on the check." According to McCabe, expectations play a role: "When a group of us go out, I *expect* it will cost more than my share. Frankly, I'd be uncomfortable to ask what was my exact share." McCabe also mentioned that often he is on his expense account because of the nature of his position.

Paula Kahn, New York advertising executive, is nonplussed by the issue. "In our business," she says, "we usually handle the check problem easily. Because we are on expense accounts, we take turns picking up the tab when there is not a host."

The idea of picking up tabs or splitting checks may not be a problem for anyone on an expense account, but what about the rest of us who pay our own way, whether it is a social or business meal? We don't want to appear cheap. On the other hand, the idea of forking out forty dollars for a salad and hot tea seems *very* unfair. And costly.

In addition, I learned several things after a number of calls:

● There is *no* pat solution.
● There are different mind-sets about the issue of group dining.
● There are different observations and realities for men and women:
  • Men are more often on expense accounts and expect to pick up tabs.
  • Women tend to spend more time identifying each person's total. Several women I interviewed decried the haggling they had seen. A male business associate is more understanding because "overall, women still earn less than men"!
  • Men more often expect to split bills evenly regardless of who drank the Tab. On the other hand, nobody wants to be used.

Chris Carr, meeting and convention planner for AAA, feels that the issue becomes touchy when you don't know the other diner that well. "I usually don't drink at lunch and don't feel comfortable paying my share of several people's three-martini lunches. But we split the tab because it's easier."

Chutzpah Redefined

"One time there was a group of twenty of us who went out after a meeting. One fellow drinks a liqueur that cost $25 per glass and had five rounds. He managed to be on the dance floor when the bill arrived!"

That fellow is a *major* contender for the chutzpah*
award. But he has lots of competition. One professional said
her ire was up the evening she and five colleagues went to
dinner. One of them was a self-appointed wine connoisseur
who felt compelled to order a $75 bottle for everyone to
share (both in sips and cents), "and most of us couldn't tell
the difference between a $7 bottle and the $75 one!"

According to my informal survey, picking up the tab was
not a problem when it was clear that the person who
extended the invitation was the host. The dining experience
became an issue when there was no designated host.

While having dinner in San Francisco with my friend of
thirty-five years, Pam Massarksy, an officer for the Chicago
Teachers Union, I heard another side of the issue. "My
husband, David [Peterson], lobbyist for the Chicago Teachers
Union, *loves* to eat when we go out to dinner. He eats a full
seven-course meal, has three martinis, wine and after-dinner
drinks. He *refuses* to split the tab because he doesn't want to
feel constrained by the person who has a piece of fish with a
cup of coffee. David handles this by saying up-front to our
dinner companions, 'You just pay for what your share is; we
are *not* splitting the tab.' And he pays the rest."

Being up-front is the key. There are many people who
do not drink. Noah Griffin is one of them. "When I go out
with other people, I say up-front that I am happy to split the
food tab, but I don't drink. Nobody has ever complained or
refused to include me at dinner."

A "Host" of Solutions

Some proposed solutions to the dilemma:

1. Ask whether the meal is hosted, Dutch or split.
   Dutch—pay your own way (this often becomes a split).
   Split—divided evenly.
   Host—tab is picked up.
   Make your decision accordingly on joining the group.

*See Glossary.

2. Barry Wishner shared his late father's method: "Be conscious of the price of the meal and libations. Add twenty percent tip and tax plus an extra *five dollars* as soon as the check is put on the table, which keeps anyone from being stuck with uncalculated extras." One woman I know told me she always gives her exact amount so she never feels ripped off. But her mealmates do if the "exact amount" is less than adequate for her share, and it always is.

3. If you are the guest, don't take advantage.

4. A word to the offenders who order the most expensive food and a number of drinks and costly wine: A lot of us have your number, even if we suffer silently at the table. You can bet, tomorrow we are burning up the wires with the word on you! The network works in mysterious ways. Take a hint from David Peterson: Offer to pay the full amount you have incurred!

5. Another solution is to choose restaurants that will give separate checks. This may be a problem for the server and/or restaurant, but it surely makes sense to ask. In this case, a twenty percent tip is in order.

A number of people mentioned another irritating issue: the person who picks up the tab, charges it, collects everyone's cash, and then keeps the receipt and deducts the entire meal. One fellow said he almost felt compelled to call the IRS and give them an anonymous tip.

Remember:

- Breaking bread may make or break your business!
- Dining know-how is a nuance of networking.
- Make it your business to avoid being a real meal schlemiel.*
- E.T. may phone home after lunch, but not during it.

*See Glossary.

Reminders

➤ Business lunch is a quasi-social/business event requiring a working knowledge of etiquette. Power and control plays have their place in mega-meals when negotiating for mega-deals. However, these P&C antics are inappropriate in a lunch that is supposed to increase the circle of contacts and establish business relationships.

➤ Hosts have responsibilities for: prearranging specifics, seeing to the comfort of guests, contributing to the flow of conversation, setting the time parameters, and picking up the tab as inconspicuously as possible. If you are the receiver of ideas, leads, advice, or information, you are the host.

➤ Guests would be well advised to observe the host's behavior as a guideline for ordering food and drink. Have conversation prepared to contribute to the flow.

➤ The only big-time operation that requires a portable phone at lunch is a heart transplant. Unless you are the surgeon or recipient, leave the phone at the office.

➤ Splitting tabs may be a problem that can be prevented by prior planning and close communication.

➤ If one views "dinner with a gang" as an evening meal and entertainment (if the gang is entertaining), then the cost of the meal includes the show.

➤ If the budget is very lean, you can decline the invitation, rather than risk a dent in the pocket and a don't in the network.

9

▶ ▶ ▶ ▶ ▶ ▶ ▶ ▶ ▶ ▶ ▶ ▶ ▶ ▶ ▶ ▶ ▶ ▶ ▶ ▶

The Phone Factor

This chapter is not about making magical cold calls, nor is it about how to use the telephone to play power games and "phon-y" telephone tactics.

This chapter is about using the telephone to stay in touch, to follow up, and to be connected—not disconnected! There are some ideas, rules, horror stories, "phonetastic" tales, and do's and don'ts.

Today's advanced technology has complicated what was once a basic avenue of communication. People can now call from their cars, while walking down a street, in an elevator, from the bathroom, and from the bleachers at a baseball game. There are car phones, cellular phones with fax machines, portable phones, and—Lord, have mercy—videophones. It isn't enough that the phone "could be" intrusive; now we will have to look good when we are interrupted! This is a frightening thought, although not a new one. The Chicago Museum of Science and Industry had an AT&T picture phone exhibit over thirty years ago.

While technology may have complicated the phone and its usage, what remains a simple truth is that we still must mind our phone manners, and our manner in using the phone. Some folks find the phone and its proliferations—answering machines, answering services, fax machines, and new features, call-interrupt, call-forward, voice mail—to be confusing and sometimes irritating, and they are!

But the telephone offers so much more. I have always believed that my attachment to the source of nourishment in life was a telephone cord, not the umbilical cord! It may be that my positive attitude has permitted me to make the phone my friend...and to be a phone friend. Research shows that people who have relaxed phone conversations with friends are happier. So there!

With that attitude, we can touch base with our networks, solve problems, and increase our resource base. Today's economy requires us to be effective, efficient, and connected. The telephone helps us meet those requirements.

The Revolt Against the Revolution

The telephone revolutionized communication and, almost one hundred years later, has precipitated a new revolt. The invention, once so highly valued, is now being viewed with the derision and scorn better suited to a plague of sewer rats. Nonetheless, I protest! The telephone is the tool that keeps us *connected* to colleagues, family, and friends. While we send cards and faxes, write notes and letters (an endangered species of communication), the telephone is a special communication tool. When face-to-face conversations are impossible, the phone is the best interactive technological tool. It affords us the opportunity to "learn by hearing" another's conversational style (tone, pace, inflection), to intuit the emotions, and to respond appropriately. We do get to "reach out and touch someone."

According to author/humorist Fran Liebowitz, "The telephone is a good way to talk to people without having to offer them a drink."

The Telephone Tree of Life

The telephone tree is a concept that has been used for many years. We had one for our high school club to notify members of changes in meeting dates or locations. The telephone tree allows people to share in the process of getting messages through organizations.

But the telephone tree has also been the "Tree of Life" for Cheryl Matsuno, a podiatric medical assistant and avid horsewoman. "We were riding the trails through Marin when my horse got skittish, threw me, and stepped on me, resulting in a lacerated liver. I was in intensive care for seventeen days and required fifty pints of blood. The people in my horse world, social world, old friends from high school, my mother's friends, our patients at the clinic, and friends of friends all responded by each giving me a pint of blood. I am alive today because of the telephone and my extended network of generous, caring people."

The Telephone as a Problem-Solver, Not Just the Problem

Some people treat the phone as a major problem. I agreed to sit on a panel on publishing at a speakers' convention and present a ten-minute spiel. At the time, it sounded like a good idea. But with the deadline for this book fast approaching, it no longer was. I solicited feedback from two of my valued colleagues and called to explain my dilemma to the friend who had recommended me. She gave me her support for withdrawing and also suggested I call our colleague Allen Klein, speaker and author. I did and he consented to replace me. Then I called our workshop chair, who was delighted that Allen would participate.

Some busy people might consider the time I invested in resolving this issue a monumental waste. I disagree. Feeling conflicted by mutually exclusive commitments was a waste of time. Taking the time to resolve the issue was not. The problem was solved and the acknowledgements made by 8:45 A.M. It took twenty minutes and saved me three days...for writing!

Ten calls, a problem solved, and a true story for this chapter. Such a deal!

Managing Moments and Minutiae

The beauty of the telephone is that it is a two-way (or more) means of communication. But for some of us, the interactive nature of the phone is its biggest liability. In an era when MANAGING MOMENTS is valued as the timesaving tip for ultimate career success, having to participate in an actual conversation is considered wasteful. Why? There are several possible reasons:

1. Some people don't consider themselves good conversationalists, so they choose not to struggle.
2. Some people fear rejection. "I used to be so very intimidated by the phone twenty years ago, fearing possible rejection," revealed Ruthe Hirsch, a consultant who assists older adults making lifestyle transitions. "I observed a colleague place phone calls with ease; he was having a good time talking to people. I followed his example. Now I talk on the phone to *people*—not to contacts—and consider the phone (my instrument of choice) a valuable tool."
3. People communicate differently, which leads to misunderstandings.
4. Some people think they are too busy (important) to waste one moment on anyone else.

There are as many reasons as there are people who shy away from the phone.

Sheer Hear-esy!

While all the busy people are managing their moments on the phone as a timesaving technique, dare to be different. **Don't save nanoseconds.** Spend a moment making small talk. Invest a minute or two in having conversation that contributes to rapport.

When you receive a call that is ill timed, say so and offer a time that is better.

Waste your time! If you're placing or receiving a call that follows a meeting or an event; invest your time and show interest. The risk: You'll "lose" a few minutes. The rewards: You'll increase your network, resources, information base, power, and circle of influence. Maybe you'll find a tennis partner, a job lead, a fellow philosopher, or even...a friend!

Several years ago as part of my marketing plan, I mailed letters to Chicago-based Meeting Planners who had conventions scheduled for San Francisco. There was a method to my madness! I was going back to Chicago for my twenty-year high school reunion and planned on combining business with pleasure. After the reunion I placed several calls, one to Kathleen Goldsmith of the American College of Surgeons. After I introduced myself and referred to my letter, I added, "I am here in Chicago for my twenty-year reunion, which was an incredible experience and such fun!" Kathleen, a friendly and charming person, immediately asked which high school it was and where the reunion was held. She took the time to respond, which furthered our exchange of small talk and allowed us to discover mutual interests.

Although she had already hired other speakers for the convention that year, she asked me to periodically keep in touch, which I did. She has since hired me to speak at two conventions, and a third speaking engagement is on the books. And her endorsement quote is on my first book, *How to Work a Room*. Over the years we have become phone friends who get together when we are in Chicago or San Francisco. Small talk has big payoffs.

Touching Base

Touching base is as critical for us as for the baseball player who tags each base as he rounds the diamond toward home plate.

Rule: IF YOU DON'T TOUCH BASE, YOU CAN GET THROWN OUT OF THE GAME!

There is no network of contacts or resource base available to you if you do not touch base. You drop yourself out of people's lives and Rolodexes.™ You can drop back in, but it is infinitely more difficult.

Rule: TOUCH BASE WHEN YOU NEED NOTHING!

We all know people who call periodically, sound extremely friendly and personable, and then—the slam dunk— they ask for a favor. There are several people with whom I am friendly, but they are not my friends. There is a qualitative difference. One reason: They only call for their benefit and have *never* called just to say hello.

Cut to the Chase

Mark Chimsky, editor in chief of Collier Books, a division of Macmillan Publishing, is so friendly and personable that we became phone friends a year before we met. "The other day," Chimsky said, "a former colleague of mine called and spent fifteen minutes schmoozing.* I hadn't heard from him in over a year, and I thought maybe he was just being friendly. But then he asked for a big favor. My advice: Cut to the chase. A few pleasantries are fine, but to mislead me to think this was a friendship call when there is an agenda does not work for me. I would have preferred it if he had asked his favor two minutes into the conversation." Mark, good-natured as he is, felt he was misled and used.

*See Glossary.

Rule: IF YOU ONLY TOUCH BASE TO SATISFY YOUR INTERESTS, YOUR RESOURCES WILL DRY UP.

Farrell Chiles, trainer and consultant, has always called just to say hello. "How else do you keep 'connected' to people if you never talk to them?" he asked rhetorically.

George Walther, author of best-seller *Phone Power,*[23] adds that "communicating useful information in business... requires us to get to the meat of the message. To be perceived as a sharp thinker, get to the point." We can assist the caller in doing so by asking, "How may I help you?" In a more informal call, a simple "What's up?" suffices.

In the early eighties, the *San Francisco Examiner* featured a weekly column on careers. As the consulting coordinator and a frequent contributor I often received queries from interested writers. One of these persons had met me through mutual acquaintances and decided to "befriend" me. Her ploy was "Let me share my vast resources with you, and you can do the same." She called several times and each time I stopped what I was doing and responded. Twice she stopped me in midsentence and said, "Susan, that is not on *my* agenda." Some would consider this "communications/ political deal maker" a terrific time manager, but not I. She neglected to value *my time,* and consequently, she didn't manage her manners. For that, there is no excuse.

The truth is that all people are busy with the demands of the job, community, and professional organizations, as well as a personal and family life. What will distinguish us is *how* we handle that busyness.

Because she is so friendly and warm on the phone, I asked Shayna Stillman of National Speakers Forum what makes it so easy for her to meet people on the phone. "When someone sounds genuinely pleased to talk to me, I respond in kind. If you behave enthusiastically, you'll eventually think and feel that way."

Rule: CONVEY ENTHUSIASM AND INTEREST IN THE PERSON. PAY ATTENTION.

What if you are *not* genuinely interested in calling? Then

don't. I am not talking about a callback to the IRS, which legitimately may not engender your effusive, warm greetings. We are not talking about cold calls; these are follow-up calls to someone you met or a contact someone has referred to you—warm calls.

A Slow Burn over Cold Calls

According to Kerry Davis, owner of Word Weaver secretarial service, it is very irritating to get a phone call from someone asking for the owner, manager, etc. "Because often, when I answer, 'Speaking,' the unknown caller then asks, 'What's your name?' I am immediately on the offensive, since I don't know who they are or why they want to know. I *can* immediately assume they're selling something! These people never identify themselves first. If I do mistakenly answer, 'My name's Kerry Davis,' they then reply, 'Hi, Kerry, and how are you today?' (often in a slime-laden, falsely friendly voice). I object to the false friendliness, and very much so to the familiarity. I must admit I'm not really crazy about being called Ms., Miss, or Mrs. Davis by most people, but I definitely expect it from unsolicited phone callers! I also object to their not telling me right off what they're calling about and for not asking if they're interrupting me. Then, of course, when I say, 'No, thank you very much, I'm not interested' in whatever they may be selling, they argue with me and ask all sorts of personal questions. For example, 'And what's your annual income?' Now, what could be a better way *not* to sell something than by using this method?"

Kerry, who is most gracious and makes it her business to never sound "rude, even when rushed," *has* been "sold" over the phone. "Invariably they're the people who say, 'Hello, I'm so and so, and I'm calling to see if you're interested in such and such. No? Well, thanks for your time. You might keep us in mind in the future.' Friendly, proper, short, and sweet! They don't ask me my name or anything else inappropriate!"

Doing Double Duty

One interviewee said that he called to hire a subcontractor who had submitted a proposal for a project. As they spoke, "I heard the sound of her computer keys clicking away. Her message was clear: 'My inputting is more important than your comments.' It was so discourteous, I decided to hire someone else."

Some people can do two things at once, but few of them make you feel that they are paying attention while they are doing double duty. According to Kerry Davis, patient translator of hieroglyphics (including my *handwritten* manuscript of this book), "That includes people who eat and chew while talking on the phone. The message is 'I only have time to eat...in your ear.'" This behavior gives new meaning to the idiom "He chewed my ear off."

Davis also suggests that if, while on the phone with someone, another person comes into your office with a question, do not talk to both people at once. Or don't have one of those whispered conversations on the side with one, while the other thinks he has your full attention—until he hears that whispered conversation and/or feels the loss of your attention. Excuse yourself to the caller for just a moment, handle the urgent interruption (only if it's urgent; otherwise, no one should have been rude enough to bother you when you were so obviously busy with a phone call), and then return to the phone conversation.

Be a Phone Friend

After you have worked rooms, had conversations, and exchanged cards, the followup is essential. If part of your follow-up process is a phone call, it is a warm call.

Rule: THERE IS NO WAY TO TURN A CONTACT MADE AT A MEETING, PARTY OR EVENT INTO A COLLEAGUE WITHOUT SOME FOLLOW-UP.

A note is a good start, yet it is one-way communication, as is a fax. For example: You attended a committee meeting at a local community organization, meeting the other members, listening to their ideas, and watching them interact. Perhaps one or two people stand out because of their ideas, delivery, and demeanor. There are several options:

1. Do nothing: play it safe, but there are no rewards.
2. Send a note expressing your positive reaction.
3. Pick up a phone, even if you have to leave a message on an answering machine or voice mail; your sincerity, warmth, and acknowledgement can be heard and felt!

A Stranger Calls

Several years ago I received a call from Charles Amico, a stranger who identified himself and the colleague who suggested he call me when he moved to San Francisco. He was full of vitality and spirit on the phone. We chatted about our mutual acquaintance, Charles's move, and San Francisco. As I hadn't been apprised, his call was unexpected, and turned into an unexpected pleasure. We stayed in touch, met over coffee, and became buddies. We have matching energy levels, similar pacing, tone, listening skills, and laughter levels.

Communications experts conclude that these similarities create the basis for the comfort that contributes to rapport. There are people who advocate deliberately mimicking or mirroring other people to "create rapport." I am uncomfortable with the concept when it is taken to the extreme. The statement that comes to mind is "To thine own self be true." What if you are at an event talking to a group with three people of differing communication personalities and styles? Whom do you mirror without sounding like Rich Little?

While it makes sense to listen and to play attention to tone, pacing, inflection, and energy, don't be a mimic, be yourself. After all, you are the person with whom your contacts will have to interact. It is, in the long run, easiest to be yourself, and it saves time. You'll never have to remember to be anyone but yourself.

Effective Phone Lines

When calling at the behest of another person, for starters:

1. Identify yourself.
2. Name the person whom you are calling.
3. State the name of the connection.

"Hello, may I please speak to Jane Jones? This is Sarah Bernhardt. Elmer Fudd suggested that I call."

Be sure to thank the secretary for his/her part.

If you do reach Jane, you introduce yourself—with energy and a smile in your voice.

The next statement is crucial, and shows regard for Jane Jones:

Always ask, **"Is this a good time?"** "If not now, when would be a good time?"

If Jane has only two minutes, promise brevity and deliver it.

Convey the positive comments your mutual contact has said about Jane: "Elmer said you are one of the most knowledgeable people in the industry."

It's the truth and it is about her and could help make Jane feel more at ease and receptive. Write a follow-up note to Jane acknowledging the time and information shared. And a note to Elmer!

Knowledgeable networkers acknowledge! Apprise everyone involved of the progress of the connection.

A Word About Secretaries and Assistants

Secretaries and assistants work with their bosses and they have a routine established for screening and placing calls. Being short or too insistent with the secretary rarely has a payoff. You may get through now, but you may lose the connection long-term. As Carl LaMell advises: "Remember, the assistant and the boss are a team."

Pleasant, considerate communication with the secretary or assistant can only reflect positively on you. If Jane Jones had indicated that Thursday would be better, you could offer to call at a convenient time on Thursday. Then do so. The opener is: "I am Sarah Bernhardt. Jane Jones is expecting my call. We met last week at a fund-raiser for the Leukemia Society." Give enough information to help Jane Jones remember you.

Try to be light-hearted when calling because most people are efficient and serious. So do the opposite. Use a mirror to make sure there is a smile on your face and transfer it to your voice. Pay attention to the voice on the other end. Is there stress or urgency? Ask if this is a good time; if the answer is yes, ask about the weather, or offer a comment about sports or events. Our 7.1 earthquake in the San Francisco Bay Area and the fire storm in Oakland gave us something to talk about with strangers!

How do you know where to draw the line so that a friendly phone call does not become overfriendly? Listen. Pay attention to the cues, pauses, pace, and tone so that you'll be mindful of people's time.

Telephone Terminator

If starting a phone conversation is not easy, ending it may be tougher. One of the memorable phone call closers was my grandmother, an immigrant whose imperfect English was her second language. When she was ready to get off the phone, she did! In her warmest grandmotherly tone, she'd say, "Thank you *so much* for calling." *Click*. She hung up. That was that! (But she made a chopped liver that more than redeemed her chopped-off conversation!)

Miss Manners suggests that the originator of the call is

supposed to end it, but "if the limits of human endurance are reached, the recipient may. One terminates a call by changing to a hearty voice and saying, 'Well, good,' followed by a summary, 'I'm glad to hear you closed the deal,' or 'See you Friday.' Then: 'Goodbye.' "[24]

One of the best phone call closings happened as I was drafting this chapter. It struck me as being so thoughtful and considerate that the goodbye felt good. Sheldon Baker, a public relations professional and buddy, is handling my publicity. He is always prepared with the material we need to discuss before he calls. One time we talked during a "writing day." His exact words: "Susan, I really appreciate the time you've taken while being under the gun [book deadline]. Though our calls are sometimes lengthy, I value the time you've given."

He could have said, "I have ten more clients to call. Got to go." But he didn't. Sheldon Baker's voice and tone *supported* his words. As he ended our conversation, I felt good. It can be done.

Telephone Tag: Reach Out, but Don't Touch

I had recently received a call from a "champion telephone tagger" who was disappointed that she actually got me and not my machine. She placed her call at 6:15 P.M., hoping to leave the message that another speaker had been chosen for the conference. This same person had contacted me, and was oh so "delighted that I had personally and promptly returned her call." But she preferred to be impersonal with the rejection.

Some messages don't require a conversation: a confirmation of a meeting, a change in lunch date location, reminder to stop by the dry cleaner on the way home. For that, answering machines and voice mail serve a purpose. Debby Love-Sudduth of Apple Computer finds that she has "resolved many problems successfully via answering machines."

Some messages preclude the use of technology and

require the participation of both parties, no matter how busy or important you think you are.

A friend suffered a disturbing symptom that rendered her anemic and often immobile. She found a doctor with appropriate medical expertise and shortly after a consultation returned home to find this message from the doctor on her answering machine: "If the medicine I prescribed doesn't work, you'll have to have a hysterectomy." My friend was shaken by the news and appalled that she learned it from an answering machine. The doctor may know medicine, may even have a bedside manner, but obviously not telephone sense.

Syndicated columnist Ellen Goodman captured the essence of phone power plays in a column called "Telephone Tag of the '90s: Not Talking to a Person, a Time-saving Technique, Is the Goal."[25]

Goodman reveals that she doesn't know the "precise" etiquette of telephone tag. She is not alone; no one does. What still prevails is the C^2 Test: Is it Courteous or not, and Considerate or not? Hearing of potential surgery, a canceled deal, retracted job offer, or any bad news via technology is not appropriate. If the only merit is that the behavior in question is expeditious—a real timesaver—then it receives a demerit.

If you are one who believes, as Goodman says, that "haste has become the new status symbol; talking is considered wasteful," then you will be out of touch, decreasing your network resources and base of referrals.

You "Auto" Give Us a Call

Car phones can really be a "blessing." A Friday afternoon outdoor wedding in Tel Aviv almost didn't take place. Sundown was fast approaching and the rabbi was late. One of the guests called a friend, the chief rabbi of a nearby town, who empowered a guest to conduct the ceremony via car phone (*Marin Independent Journal*). The scene does activate the imagination. What if the car phone had call-waiting? Would the bride and groom be left "call-waiting at the altar"?

Car phones are a time- and lifesaver. But they, too, must be used appropriately. Very important calls that require excellent clarity may be ill suited for a car phone. Although technology continues to improve, the transmission of a call as the car enters a tunnel does not! One would hate to be in the midst of the important deal-clinching exchange only to have the line go dead...and maybe the deal with it. Drive time is a good time to make calls, as long as driving conditions are heeded and conversations are *not* heated.

Pepper . . . and Salt

THE WALL STREET JOURNAL

"Why don't we call our car phone, and when we hear the ring we'll remember where we parked."

From the *Wall Street Journal*—Permission, Cartoon Features Syndicate

Setting priorities is an oft-heard phrase and very savvy advice. An interviewee was on a business trip and was visiting with a long-time friend. "My friend is very busy and works full-time so that Saturday I had to share her with the electrician, which was understandable. And I knew we'd have some time alone in the car as she dropped me off. Wrong! No sooner did we back out of her driveway than her car phone rang. It was her mother. It rang again; this time it was her sister, to whom she had spoken two hours earlier. The third time it rang I spoke up and told her to get off the phone because she hadn't spent ten minutes in an hour conversing with me." Her implicit message was clear; "My arrangements to go to the jeweler are far more important than your visit."

Back to Basics

It is worth rethinking the issues of manners and etiquette as we use the Tools and Toys of Technology. The basic questions remain: Is it courteous? Is it considerate?

It is also important to be aware of the implicit messages we give. Does our behavior reflect respect for the other person? Or the opposite? This does not refer to coping with telephone canvassing calls from strangers. Bills are being considered in several states to eliminate the invasion of home privacy.

Portable Rudeness

I've been told many horror stories by people who attended plays and operas and dined in the better restaurants only to have the event interrupted by beepers, portable phones, and watch alarms. Is that showing respect or showing off?

No one pays money to attend an event or dine in a relaxing atmosphere to have it disturbed. My friends Kadi Yamamoto and Brian Kay returned from living in Hong Kong, thrilled to be able to dine in restaurants in peace. The restaurant reviews in Hong Kong now include a phone-to-table ratio so that diners may choose a potentially quieter atmosphere. In Hong Kong, there are so many portable phones that even the children carry them.

We have always given leeway to medical doctors who tend to life-threatening situations. And the medical profession has found ways to be reached in theaters, restaurants, and parties without being disruptive. If you must wear a beeper, wear a vibrating one, as does one of my buddies. Get a charge from your voice-mail messages, and don't disturb us!

A keynote speaker was addressing an audience of three hundred interior designers when in midsentence she heard a phone ring loudly. Knowing everyone else heard the ringing, she responded by saying, "If a phone did not ring, then I just learned I have tinnitus." The audience laughed, and the speaker asked the phone-carrier to stand and introduce himself, as he already had the floor. "I made a judgement call, but all I could think was how someone could be (a) so misguided in their self-importance and (b) so rude," shared the stunned presenter whose humor saved the speech.

Check your phones at the door or leave them in your car.

Speaking Against Speakerphones

If you need your hands free, use a headset. Speakerphones often don't pick up voices if one is too far across the room or one's head is turned away from the mic. Or they can produce an echo that makes it difficult to hear the speaker on either end of the line. Sometimes, due to the echoing back of your voice, there can also be the uncomfortable feeling (paranoia?) by the person on the nonspeakerphone end of the line that a large audience has gathered at the other end to eavesdrop on what may be a private conversation. Speakerphones are also tough on the vocal cords.

The Wonders of Call-Waiting

Many rejoiced at the news that the busy signal had been laid to rest. For entrepreneurs with small businesses and without a full-time secretary, this was a boon, which eventually is going bust! The frustration of hearing a busy signal was replaced with the frustration of deciding which call was more important: the conversation with a potential client or the call from cousin Willie the Welsher? Mother or mother-in-law? Call from Ed McMahon informing you of your sweepstakes prize or the telemarketing department of your local newspaper?

Bizarro cartoon reprinted by permission
of Chronicle Features, SF, CA by Dan Piraro

There are times when people who have several phone lines will say, "I have a long-distance call from Tokyo that I must take." It makes sense, no offense taken. Call-waiting operates the same way.

Miss Manners lauded the busy signal as an inexpensive method of informing callers that we are already in conversation.[26]

Use a second phone line for outgoing calls. If that is not possible, and if a conversation is urgent and should not be interrupted, disconnect call-waiting before you call. Incoming calls can be free of call-waiting by buying the three-way calling feature. Because of the radio interviews that I give, this feature has been invaluable.

Radio Rude

Again, some people are so hooked to their phones that they do *strange* things. Talk-show host and author Judith Briles was conducting a live remote radio interview with a very animated and interesting guest. "In the middle of our live interview, we heard her call-waiting signal. I was stunned when she actually put me *and* our live interview on hold to take the other call! After the show, I apprised her of the inappropriateness of her decision." We are not sure whether this is a sign of rudeness, chutzpah, or downright ignorance.

Miss Manners reminds us all of the high consideration quotient for original callers. Interruptions should be acknowledged and that call returned once you have politely finished with caller number one. Friends may have an understanding that social chats during work hours are curtailed by incoming business calls. But once you have said, "I'll get back to you," do so.

The Return of the Phone Call

Do it. Prioritize calls, pick a good time to make calls, then have materials prepared that you might need, and pick up the phone. Do it in as timely a fashion as possible.

Letitia Baldridge recommends that corporate executives place their own calls, return calls within twenty-four hours, and should not have their calls screened.

Robin Cantor-Cooke, free-lance audiotape producer, called one day in shock. She had an etiquette question about her upcoming wedding and called Ms. Baldridge in New York, expecting to speak to an assistant. Lo and behold, Letitia Baldridge answered the phone and spent ten minutes answering Robin's question. She *does* practice what she recommends.

If you are facing a deadline and are literally swamped, delegate the call.

The Point of No Return

There may be times when you know the person who called and absolutely want *nothing* to do with the person. A colleague struggled with the phone message of someone whom he had known for five years and absolutely recoiled at the thought of any conversation. "I chose not to call, which is one of the bonuses of being an entrepreneur and choosing clients. There were no contracts or monies on the table, because I knew this person long enough and well enough to know I would not be associated with him." We do get to exercise caution and judgement when there is enough data in that casts a shadow. Not returning a call is an option, but one that should be carefully reviewed.

Be a Two-timer

The above situation creates a dilemma for the caller. You meet a person at a Chamber of Commerce luncheon. The conversation was pleasant and you decide to follow up with a call...and leave a message. No response. What to do? Be a two-timer. Try a second time. Messages get misplaced, machines garble and glitch.

If there is no return call this time, assess your purpose.

Did you call to score a business deal? Or to say you enjoyed the conversation? We signal our intentions to others and sometimes that doesn't work for the other party.

Send a handwritten note that conveys your positive thoughts. Then let it go. The time may not be right, nor the person interested in further communication. Maybe that person is out of the country. According to the laws of chance, there are enough interested people whom you've met who will respond. Pay attention to them. As hard as it is to believe, not everyone is in the market for our products, services, or our acquaintance.

Voice Maelstrom

If the scourge of modern communication is voice mail, then the hero is Ed Cruchfield, chairman of First Union Bank in Charlotte, North Carolina, who disconnected his to the applause of his employees.[27] There is voice mail and voice maelstrom; the former replicates an answering machine and is one-to-one communication. This system works well at Travel Advisers in Mill Valley, where my friend Lisa Miller handles my travel needs. The receptionist checks to see if Lisa is on a call and asks, "Would you like me to take a message or connect you to voice mail?" Callers are given a choice.

Then there is voice maelstrom. In pursuit of the most current data for this chapter, I tried calling the marketing director for Pacific Bell Voice Mail. John Flinn's *San Francisco Examiner* article had indicated that a "Voice Mail Etiquette Booklet" was in the process of being written, and I wanted a copy. But I had to endure the PacBell process of voice mail to get the booklet.

If voice mail irritates you, you are not alone. New research conducted at Stanford University indicates that "the technology violates basic rules of communication," according to Clifford Moss, assistant professor of communications at Stanford. "Hearing a human voice, even a recorded one, triggers the expectation that the voice at the other end will *pay attention* to us. Voice mail does not do any of these things. It's a quasi-conversation that violates all rules of conversation."[28] We don't like having our rules violated by anyone or anything.

As a consumer, I dislike voice mail. As an individual, I like leaving a direct message on voice mail or an answering machine. Debby Love-Sudduth of Apple Computer finds "nothing more frustrating than not being able to leave a message or to do so with someone who can't communicate the message adequately."[29]

Confirming Connections: Fabulous Follow-up

The follow-up that cements connections is two-way communication. While machines, voice mail, E-mail, and fax transmissions impact information, they are one-dimensional and without tone, spirit, or shared laughter. Melinda Henning, founder of Doing Business by Phone™, has shared the following tips for confirming connections through voice mail or answering machines.

1. The beep indicates that you now have your contact's attention and the chance to make an impact with your message.
2. Call as soon as possible after the meeting to leave a message, just as you might follow up with a note in a timely manner.
3. **Always** leave a message. Don't waste the call. Always include the reason for the call (and a reason to return it, if you want a return call), and **always** leave your phone number.
4. Organize your message like a voice memo, announcing its contents or purpose first.
5. Try something different. Be spontaneous and entertaining. Yours will be the only voice-mail message your contact gets that day that isn't boring.
6. Don't worry about mistakes. They make you sound real.
7. On your own voice mail, record a greeting in your own

voice that is brief but current, and lets the caller know when a callback might be expected. Encourage callers to leave a detailed message and tell them how long they have to talk.

8. Polish your vocal image as well as you do your visual image. Start smiling *before* you pick up the phone. Warm up your voice by singing low notes. To help sharpen your articulation, do "rubber face" exercises and stretch out your jaw muscles with a big yawn. To inject some energy, stand up, gesture, look in a mirror, and adopt an attitude of fun.

The Fax Facts

The fax machine is the microwave of the office, a necessity. While it has been critical for business, it's also a fun way to stay in touch...with the network. I send and receive cartoons and jokes, contracts, speaker bio sheets, and articles of interest.

There are some Commonsense Rules for Faxing:

• Be sure your light-hearted faxes are welcomed in an office setting.
• Be aware that there is no privacy on a fax machine to the office.
• Be considerate of the faxee. If you want to send your material, get permission.

The owner of a West Coast speakers' bureau was appalled at an unsolicited fax she received. "A speaker from the Midwest wanted me to have his [nonurgent] material so that I could book him for speaking engagements. I found a twelve-page fax from him and about him. He could have mailed the material rather than wasting my fax paper with his facts. I was irritated with his presumptuous action and will not risk proposing him to my clients."

E-Mail Does Not Stand for Excellence

The computer and its technological advances have given us electronic mail, which requires its own form of etiquette. There are advantages and disadvantages to sending messages over computer terminals. Mail can be sent and received anytime that is convenient for the sender and receiver. "It allows a different dimension of personality to the person only known through E-mail," according to Love-Sudduth. "The disadvantage is that there is no direct personal interaction. Sometimes a 'hot potato' E-mail message is passed around and the last person has to deal with it."

Some rules for E-mail:

1. Use the rules for written correspondence. Follow grammar, spelling, and punctuation rules.
2. Use both lower- and uppercase letters.[30]
3. Give memos a heading.
4. Sign your memos.
5. Check for "tone" of message...written communication is not accompanied by a tone of voice. Neither be too strident nor too Milquetoast.
6. Send your message to the right person.
7. Make sure it is appropriate to send your message to that person. (An interviewee said he was so pleased about setting up his nice new computer, modem, and software that he was going to send a message to a buddy. After reading an article on the number of inappropriately sent messages, he changed his mind and sent a note. Another interviewee decried the number of unsolicited E-mail messages she gets from "strangers in the corporation. If one more person sends me a message that they have an extra ticket to a Giants' game...")
8. Keep messages professional because they can be retrieved and shared.

E-mail can enhance personal networking. Karen, an employee in the Silicon Valley, was reviewing her options at a computer corporation. She sent fifty cronies at the company a message to that effect on a Sunday night. By Tuesday morning she had received a message about an available position in another division. However, two people responded by questioning the impersonal nature of the message. Friendship not only merits a personal touch but also requires it.

There are many ways to stay in touch with people. Perhaps I am old-fashioned, but it's time to return to conversation: people talking *with* not *at* each other through technology. The telephone network system, when used properly, enhances both professional and personal networking. It allows us to have access to and to be part of a greater global grapevine.

Reminders

➤ The telephone is a two-way interactive communication tool that assists us in staying connected to our network, solving problems, and increasing our resources.

➤ We must mind our phone manners when we place a call, leave a message, receive a call, retrieve a call, return it, and when we use faxes, E-mail, and voice mail.

➤ Clarity of tone, message, and information are important.

➤ Respect the rights of others before you bring your portable phone to a restaurant, ballet or baseball game.

➤ Be prepared for the calls you place. Make sure there is a smile on your face that is reflected in your voice.

➤ Be sure your phone tone, voice, and inflections reflect your words. "I *liked* your ideas for our fund-raiser" must sound enthusiastic, not deadpan.

➤ Don't let your need to be constantly available and in touch show you are out of touch with etiquette.

10

▷▷▷▷▷▷▷▷▷▷▷▷▷▷▷▷▷

The Grapevine Is a Goldmine

Whenever I hear someone discount the "grapevine" and/or gossip, my ears prick up, as it is a red flag for me. I listen very carefully to what he/she has to say, because many of the people who stridently lambaste the grapevine are the very people who contribute to it. Or they are so completely out of touch with the reality of their various worlds that they are unsavvy and uninteresting—to me.

On the other hand, if used properly, the grapevine can be a powerful resource and career aid. (In my Chicago neighborhood, it was the Concord grapevine!) According to Marilyn Moats Kennedy in *Office Politics,* the grapevine is nothing more than an informal communications network.

Information Management

Savvy people realize how important informal information is. The grapevine can provide you with a great deal of useful information, especially rumors and opinions, as well as facts of the goings-on in your office, profession or network. Some people refuse to deal with the grapevine because they consider it gossip, irrelevant and beneath them. It is idle chatter for which busy, hardworking people do not have time.

If you share these reactions, consider this:

• Informal information is not necessarily personal, vicious gossip. I am not in support of listening to or passing on vicious, unsubstantiated comments or hypotheses. (Eighty percent of information in the office grapevine is business-related office politics.)
• Gossip can be an intentional leak of information that you *should* know.
• Conveying a superior attitude about the grapevine could eliminate your sources of information.
• Busy people are not necessarily hardworking. Smart people make time to manage their careers. Cultivating sources of information makes sense. We are then in a position to make informed choices based on data learned from the network.

Broadcast News

Traditionally, the grapevine has served several useful purposes. It circulates information about awards, promotions, families, illnesses, and deaths. That, of course, allows individuals, or groups, to respond accordingly.

We all have stories of hearing—through the grapevine—of a colleague's impending marriage, the boss's daughter's graduation with honors, the death of a competitor's child, or a client receiving an outstanding volunteer award from the local Chamber of Commerce or Heart Association. We have then sent a wedding, graduation, sympathy, or congratulatory card—or called to convey our message. Is the recipient offended because the information was passed on through the networks? No. On the contrary.

In Sympathy

Judith Briles, keynote speaker and prolific author (*The Confidence Factor, Dollars & Sense of Divorce, Woman to Woman: From Sabotage to Support*), lost her son Frank, who was nineteen years old. She has since written her story in a beautiful book, *When God Says No* (Word Publishing). At the time of Frank's death, she received cards, calls, and letters from numerous colleagues, clients, associates, and some old adversaries. In Judith Briles's time of grief, her adversaries learned of her loss through the grapevine and newspapers, and responded in support.

Judith was very surprised: "I called and thanked them for their expressions of sympathy. It didn't resolve the old differences but there was interaction on another plateau. In my time of grief, our differences were put into the perspective that the death of a child brings to light."

Gentle Reminder

This is a good time to reiterate and expand a basic premise: Knowledgeable networkers acknowledge. This also includes those events of daily living of others: our friends, acquaintances, clients, and competitors. If writing notes expressing sympathy, congratulations, and so forth is not your forte, delegate that task to the greeting card industry. That industry has risen to every occasion! A visit to your local card shop will prove my point...and will provide a few hearty laughs, as many of the cards are so funny.

People do remember those people who took the time to reach out in their moment of joy or grief. Thoughtful people make time. Whether you believe in karma or in "what goes around comes around," the principle is the same. When you make time, you make memories, and good deeds are appreciated and returned at a much-needed moment.

Gripe Juice

To reiterate, those who convey a smug attitude about gossip and the grapevine discount an important resource. Over time, those sources could dry up. While hanging out at the office water cooler for hours is not recommended, taking the time to cultivate and encourage those sources of information is a smart career management move.

Michael Korda, author of *Power and Success,* has stated that gossip is a kind of informal polling system which allows management a chance to test reactions.

The grapevine also may forecast events through leaks to provide "news of the future," which you may need to know! Rumors move exceptionally fast when layoffs, furloughs or mergers are pending. Sometimes these rumors are planted to soften the blow or to take pressure off the manager who has to implement the cutbacks or firings.

To be caught off guard is very disconcerting. Some people ignore signals or don't decipher their meaning. Ignoring or discounting information could be disastrous to you and your career. Having this information, however, could benefit you tremendously. You'll be forewarned so that you can ask the right questions and observe managers, board members, and the CEO. You may even see it as a signal to update your résumé, identify your network of contacts, and get back into circulation. Actually, an updated résumé should always be on hand...or on line.

A Friendly Warning

Many active professional association members can tell when the industry has rough times...attendance at monthly meetings increases. People understand that the demands of a job (career) may be all-consuming, but the stalwarts who are the backbone of an association may be less inclined to share leads and resources if you show up just because you get wind of an impending layoff.

Stay Tuned

The premise of this book: *Stay in circulation,* even when everything is rosy in the workplace. Your potential plight will be met with more support, ideas, and referrals.

Having a diverse network that reflects our workplace and community is a plus. According to Max De Pree, "recognizing diversity in corporate life helps us to connect with the great variety people bring."[31]

Crucial Cautions

There are two crucial cautions to heed when using the grapevine:

• Listen actively
• Don't add grist for the rumor mill—it could come back to haunt you.

In addition, you'll want to respond carefully when you hear grapevine information. Your reaction to such news could be misinterpreted. I learned that from my dear friend Gertrude Gurd, confidential secretary to my big boss (then superintendent of San Francisco schools, the late Robert Alioto), who shared her wisdom with me many years ago.

In my former life as an educator, I was returning to work after a seven-month leave necessitated by a car accident. "Susan, be careful around the people you listen to who are bad-mouthing your colleagues. Any harmless acknowledge-ment, whether it's verbal or just a nod of your head, and that piece of news travels its course—and may be attributed to you," advised Gertrude. "Even silence may be misinterpreted as approval." In some cases where a vicious tidbit is mentioned, we must not give silent approval. It takes courage to "stand up and be counted." It's a decision to be made case by case.

Network News

There is a great difference between vicious gossip and shared tidbits (or bytes) of negative information. Be careful about that which you enter in your computer. Remember Bryant Gumbel's gaffe? As I was writing (yes, *writing* by hand) the above sentence, the phone rang. A dear friend and colleague shared that the public relations director for a publishing house, known to her to have questionable practices, had joined a publishing house of my acquaintance— also with questionable practices. Shared juicy information, plucked from the vine, inspiring my friend to comment, "Water seeks its own level." Shared laughter, and back to the grindstone. The pause that refreshes, and informs! Network news transmitted. More important, it was a piece of information that I should know, as it has some potential impact on me as an author. Information is power.

Keep in mind, one never knows when one will hear important news through the grapevine. How many times have we thought of terrific responses an hour later? Studies indicate that top achievers have a practiced response for those situations that could render them speechless.

There's another aspect of the grapevine that could pose a sticky situation. What if *you* are the target of the information tidbit that is passed through the office grapevine? You should determine if it's professional or personal in nature. Don't lose your temper, but consider:

- Tracing and confronting the source
- Approaching your boss if the grapevine indicated your job was in jeopardy
- Preparing a memo
- Ignoring the information

Only you can decide which option is appropriate. If you have a good sounding board, present your dilemma.

A former mentor advised that denying a rumor was a waste of time. Such a response could serve to "validate that rumor with those people who needed to pass on damaging information." Maybe.

There is another theory: Silent approval could also serve to validate rumors and vicious lies. History is replete with abominations that silence approved, to the detriment of those who suffered.

Information Is Power

The office or professional grapevine may be a resource or a sound alert. Marilyn Moats Kennedy suggests that some of these vocal tidbits may be "advanced information...which buys lead time...to plan a strategy."

People who are smart at managing their careers have a career plan with supportive strategies and options for Plans B and C. And they also know who has formal power, according to their positions and titles. More important, they are keenly aware of who has informal power. Talk to everyone: the secretaries, custodians, paraprofessionals. The worst thing that will happen is that you'll learn a lot—from many sources—and have many sources of support.

Smart people observe at the office, at meetings, and at office parties. They notice who laughs together. They observe facial expressions and body language, or, as someone once suggested, use the WDWTW–WWW&H formula (Who's Doing What to Whom—When, Where, Why, and How). They know who lunches, jogs, or commutes together. They listen to people to discover their values, goals, and lifestyles. They learn people's interest, such as who sails, runs, golfs, sings, or makes furniture. They know who coaches Little League and who sits on the board of the arts council.

In addition to listening and observing, smart, savvy people read. What a quaint thought! Once again, if I remind you of your fifth-grade teacher, I am guilty and delighted to do so.

We must read newspapers, business journals, trade magazines, and even books. The busy commuter can listen to audiobooks, provide the car phone isn't ringing. There is no excuse to not be in the know...now.

Information is power—well-read people are well informed. If you read the business who's who section in your local paper, trade magazines or the *Wall Street Journal,* you may learn information that merits a note or a change in tomorrow's client presentation. A client, a partner with a major East Coast law firm, reads four newspapers a day: local, the *New York Times,* the *Wall Street Journal,* and *USA Today.* He is knowledgeable and conversant.

Let your reading augment your network.

Grape Juice

If you're not already experienced at cultivating your grapevine, here are some tips:

- Determine who has access to relevant, powerful sources of information.
- Trade information when it's required
- Don't fan the flames of gossip with opinions.
- Observe your coworkers and those with whom they interact or socialize.
- Buy lunch or dinner for those who are prime grapevine sources; both inside the company and in professional associations and networks.
- Recognize that members of your professional associations may have information about your organization.
- Be aware.

The grapevine has biblical and historical roots. It has been memorialized in song by the late, great Marvin Gaye (and the California Raisins). It is here to stay. Don't waste your valuable time cursing, questioning or impugning it.

who may have informal information about your
and the profession as well.

godfather/mother mentor is distinguished from the
his or her ability to make favorable things happen
He or she is a sponsor or guide who can and will
ors for you.

do you "get" a mentor? Don't use the following tactic
on a colleague who is a senior manager. An aspiring
approached him and asked, "Would you like to be my
It sounded like "Would you be my valentine?" He said
se anyone who would ask hadn't the savvy or sense to
eneficiary of his knowledge and skills.

Mentor Traits

effective mentor should posses the following characte-

bility to teach
ledge of the organization, industry or association
willingness to share information and resources
elf-security that allows him/her to "let go" when you're
to move on or up

is last trait cannot be overemphasized because it
ts the pain of "mentor trauma." When mentoring
ships become emotional attachments, proceed with
caution.
l Gillis, president and CEO of INFO Enterprises, shares
husiasm and slightly more formalized mentor method:
ring is easily my favorite topic. I was brought up
sionally to embrace the 'each one teach one' philoso-
do not believe that one can effectively act as a mentor
asual or random basis. I believe that one cannot be
involved in mentoring, but must be committed to it.
in that I put on mentoring is perhaps a bit more
than most. Each of my protégés must:

Instead, cultivate it as a career management tool. And increase your network net worth in the process.

Recent research indicates that gossip reveals personal values and mores. Certainly it is often more purposeful than idle.

Can you afford to ignore a vast resource of information that relates to your workplace and your career? I doubt it.

One way of contributing to your information base is to have a network of MOMs (Mentors of the Moment).

Reminders

➤ The grapevine is an important source of information.
➤ Rumors, opinions, and facts are filtered through the grapevine. Rumors of impending layoffs are often planted to soften the blow.
➤ The information gleaned helps you make informed choices...and respond accordingly.
➤ Stay tuned to your sources, listen actively, and trade information when appropriate.
➤ Avoid adding grist to the rumor mill.
➤ Avoid malicious gossip or vicious lies befitting those "inquiring minds who want to know."
➤ An advantage to having access to the grapevine: If questioned about your sources, you can say—or *sing*—"I heard it through the grapevine."

11

▶▶▶▶▶▶▶▶▶▶▶▶▶▶▶▶▶

Mentor Mania

Mentors and mentoring have received a lot of press. Some would-be fast-track "stars" are thrilled with this "new" concept. Actually, mentoring has existed since Greek mythology. Mentor was not a shortcut to the executive suite, he was a *teacher* for Odysseus' son, Telemachus.

Today, it is almost as fashionable to lay claim to a mentor as it is to have a BMW or car phone with fax, all of which are life's "necessities." But seeking a mentor requires an understanding of what a mentor is, as well as a self-assessment. A mentor is a teacher, a guide, a coach, who will show you the ropes and, most important, encourage you. A nine-year-old can be a mentor to a six-year-old if he shares his insights, ideas, experiences, and knowledge.

Scanning the Networks

Mentors are in our lives. The best candidate for a mentor could be an immediate boss, a colleague in another company, an officer in your professional association, an older alumnus from an alma mater or a teacher. For Kay Amarotico, an actor

and teacher at San Francisco's Amer ter, one of her mentors, actor Sidr light, a beacon. He was our teacher i Sidney directed us in *The Cherry Orc* on his model, which is joyous and l

A mentor cannot and should n dues-paying process, but can guide yo the trail guide who points out variou best path, and identifies the stepping enough to allow you to cross the str guide cannot carry you across the st which stepping-stones to avoid. "My m cuts for doing my job, as well as imp and he introduced me to people that Brad Plumb, owner of a speakers' bure doors for the people I've mentored."

"Mentors are important. Without r never had opportunities to get networ advised John Sculley, CEO of Apple addressed a conference of six hundred A employees. "Mentoring works. I have r who are now vice presidents at Apple added.[32]

Once you have identified why you must choose which type is most appro *Glamour* career strategist Marilyn Moa *Politics,* there are five types: peer, ir competitive, and the godfather/mother.[3]

The *peer mentor* provides guidance an equal; the motivation is to build alliance *mentor* teaches informal aspects of th *retiree mentor* has a wealth of informatio risk; he or she knows "where all the bod *competitive mentor* is the person with y

compan compan

The others l for you. open d

Ho tried ou employe mentor no beca be the

An ristics:

• The
• Know
• The
• The
   read

T prevel relatic extrem

B his en "Ment profes phy. I on a merel The s forma

- Meet with me for at least an hour each month
- Report on progress from our last meeting
- Provide examples of how they are balancing personal and professional lives (often I find that too strong a bias toward work exists)
- Be prepared to discuss topics relevant to their industries and lend their own perspectives on the topic
- Provide me with their most current job evaluations
- Discuss their most pressing problems and job-related issues
- Promise to take on a minimum of three protégés themselves

"It is gratifying beyond description to pick up the phone and hear the genuine excitement in their voices as they relate recent job evaluations, promotions or salary increases. Easily, this is the most rewarding aspect of my career. It takes more time than many can, or will, give. However, knowing that I have contributed to several protégés who have earned the title of President gives me a sense of satisfaction unsurpassed by almost any other I could describe."

Bill Gillis sets an example for those of us who want to make a difference.

How to Get a Mentor

The first step in having a mentor is to observe the people around you.

- Look for the person with whom you laugh.
- Look for those treated with respect.
- Identify people "in favor."
- Don't overlook the reserved person who has much to teach.

When you have identified your chosen mentor, follow Michael Korda's advice: "Be a good listener. A surprising number of ambitious young people have never understood… [that] the art of being mentored requires that you are loyal, silent, eager to learn and willing to hold back in anticipation of future rewards."[34]

The Art of Being Mentored

Encouraging a mentoring relationship is an art that requires you to be an apt pupil. In addition, it requires sincerity, work, and the revalued trait, common sense.

Here are some strategies you can use once you have identified your potential mentor:[35]

- Smile, say "Good morning." Share observations.
- Take notice of a project that he or she has designed or completed. Send a note indicating your positive assessment of the work, planning, or outcome of the project.
- Identify some information or advice you need that your mentor candidate can provide.
- Approach your candidate and indicate your admiration of his or her work or work style.
- Ask for the help you need.
- Value the person's time and commitments. Don't consume too much work time.
- Follow up on advice or information given.
- *Report back* to your potential mentor and indicate that you are open to future advice.
- Send a personal note of thanks with an offer to host a luncheon. Call to set a date for that lunch.

Encouraging a mentoring relationship *takes time* because it must be built on trust. Allow that time, be patient and persistent. Continue to indicate that you value your potential mentor.

You can show that you are a good protégé by hard, smart work and enthusiasm.

Some other aspects of a good mentoring relationship are respect, sincerity, acknowledgement, appreciation, and practice of the Golden Rule.

Mentor Trauma: Pain and Pitfalls

Mentor trauma is one of the pitfalls of being involved with a mentor. My "femtor," the late Sally Livingston, was excellent at "letting go" with encouragement. And she was also open to the return to the nest when necessary.

Sally Livingston ushered many young entrepreneurial women along their way. She and I always laughed together, and we shared our appreciation for a really good piece of bakery-fresh rye bread, not found in abundance in the San Francisco Bay Area. The only pain was the untimely death of my fabulous femtor.

The unbearable pain of mentor trauma became obvious to me when a former mentor from my days as an educator could not cope with my evolution from schoolteacher to keynote speaker and author. His comments were biting and destructive. After trying too hard, too many times, to bridge the gap, I had to let go. In retrospect, we hardly laughed together. The one time I remember his laughter was in response to a serious comment I had made.

Choosing a mentor with a sense of security is one way to avoid the pain. Research indicates that most "successful" people have had several sponsors, people who have shared their insights, teachings, and networks. Those sponsors change as you do. My first mentor from public education, Duncan Hodel, taught me much about school board politics that continues to serve me well, but I needed different mentors as a speaker, author, and entrepreneur. It makes sense that each phase of our life requires a different support system.

But that does not mean that those people are automatically dumped once our needs change. Moving from protégé to peer to friend is possible and preferable. Peter Floyd, East Coast management consultant, has successfully made those transitions with his former mentor, the Reverend David Brown, who is now Floyd's friend. It can be done.

The best of mentors are those that embrace Socrates' attitude about his protégé, Plato: "If my student does not surpass me, then I have failed." Dr. Irving Siegel, a founding fellow of the American College of Obstetricians and Gynecologists, expected exactly that from the medical students he taught at Chicago Medical School. Unfortunately, Dr. Siegel's (and Socrates') attitude is not shared by all mentors and teachers. This can lead to traumatic transitions and sabotaged separations between mentors and protégés.

Mentor Monogamy/Serial Mentors

Times, they are a-changing. Mobility, career changes, and "downsizing" have wreaked havoc on the "safe haven for thirty years until I get the gold watch" syndrome. Consequently, the single-mentor theory is as full of holes as the single-bullet theory in the JFK assassination. We need to expand our thinking.

Although Telemachus had Mentor, King Arthur had Merlin, Muhammad Ali had Angelo Dundee, Lyndon Johnson had Sam Rayburn, we now need resource bases that are multifaceted. The concept of the mentor for life (macro-mentor) rarely applies.

I recommend that we nurture Mentors of the Moment— mini-mentors—for specific endeavors and time slots.

MOMs (Mentors of the Moment)

Dr. Michael LeBoeuf, professor, keynote speaker, and author of several best-sellers, including *Working Smart* and *GMP,* has seen his career enhanced by a series of talented individuals who have been Mentors of the Moment. "I have been very fortunate to have a network of friends and colleagues that I call on for advice and counsel. Many of these people call on me for the same. In that sense we are always mentoring each other on an as-needs basis."

LeBoeuf further explained, "Ralph Stair was a colleague from University of New Orleans who thought I could write well and encouraged me to write a book during my sabbatical. I call on Jeff Slutsky, a fellow speaker and author who shares his creative and insightful business acumen with me." LeBoeuf has created a network of friends and associates who are a source of ideas, information, assessment, and support that is reciprocal. He has been aided by his Mentors of the Moment.

MOM can even be Dad. So it is for Lee Sankowich, artistic director of Marin Theater Company, who brought *One Flew Over the Cuckoo's Nest* to the stage in the seventies. In an interview, Sankowich said, "I have had several acting coaches who have taught me my craft, but my dad was my mentor. He was a loving, gentle man who taught me to deal with others in that manner so I rarely lose my temper."

Kay Amarotico, actor and teacher at the American Conservatory Theater, considers Lee Sankowich a mentor. "He changed my professional life by casting me in *Becoming Memories*. He is gentle and lets us do what we want to do. He let us do our best and then he shaped us. The mark of a great director is that he encourages the actors. Lee Sankowich is positive with people, gives us time, and is always kind and gentle." If all the world's a stage, we can all learn a lesson from artistic director Lee Sankowich, who received his direction and mentoring from his dad from day one.

Learning is an ongoing process, and passionate protégés know this. They are inquisitive, committed, hardworking, and responsive, and drink in knowledge. "If I work with people who are open to me, I give more," Lee Sankowich adds. "Whether as a director or teacher [he taught acting at Carnegie-Mellon University], if someone is resistant, I turn off and concentrate on others."

The Professor of Football

Mentors are teachers, guides, and coaches who encourage, not bellow and belittle. The consummate mentor is coach Bill Walsh, who has trained several generations of college and professional football players. His Mentor Immortality is reflected by his protégés dominating college and professional coaching. He is a coach in the true Socratic way—allowing and encouraging his protégés to surpass him. Walsh's return to Stanford as head coach allows him to mentor the next generation in the "Walsh Ways," creating a network of coaches who will impact the future of football.

The search for the "ideal" mentor may be as consuming as the search for the ideal mate. It occurs to me that often the people who claim to be looking for Mr. or Ms. Mentor may be overlooking those people who may be Mentors of the Moment. There are many people with specific expertise who would be willing to share their knowledge.

So it was for Don Hansen, international management consultant, whose boss was his mentor. "He became a managerial role model for me, sponsoring me in various organizations, as well as my strong supporter. Though I have developed my own style, I have never forgotten his inspiring guidance, which included the advice to develop my own style."

"Though I wasn't a completely 'new kid on the block,' my mentor has helped me understand the benefits and risks related to working in different areas of the firm because she understands a lot of the politics," offered Kayla Cohen, an engineer and manager for a consulting firm.

Connection, Commonality, Chemistry

There has to be some connection between the mentor and protégé: chemistry. Although I used to believe that chemistry was instantaneous, time and experience have taught me that instant chemistry may merely be instantaneous combustion. Chemistry can develop over time in any relationship. And it can be a problem, as it was for a male attorney who had mentored a female colleague. "The relationship between a mentor and protégée can be intense and, in this case, the spontaneous combustion was a problem because we were attracted to each other," confided the attorney.

Marilyn Moats Kennedy suggests that one of the most important traits the best of mentors and protégés share is a similar sense of humor. This is an appropriate chemistry where the only aspect that is uncontrollable is the laughter—which is kosher!

Mentor Madness

What if that magical mentor chemistry develops with a boss's boss? That, too, could be problematic and has been. One interviewee, formerly with a Fortune 500 company, spoke of "the pounding" he took. Not only did his immediate superior (a term that is questionable) "resent my relationship with *his* immediate boss, but so did my peers. My mentor respected my ideas and solicited them. I, in turn, sought his guidance through the corporate maze. But the 'pounding' got to be so intolerable that I mentioned it to him. My mentor felt he could do nothing to protect me. He was eventually promoted, which made him even further away—on the organizational chart. Because he did not do anything to protect me or to help me move up the organization, I chose not to risk another layer of lumps and I had to separate from him."

This person understood the score; he had something to offer: ideas. According to Michael Korda, author and editor in chief of Simon and Schuster, "Mentoring can be seen as part of man's instinctive survival mechanism. Personal survival can depend on the same process. An older hunter needed a young man's strength for help and protection. Mentoring can be considered an early form of retirement insurance."[36]

"A mentor can either bring you up or bring you up...short," warned my corporate crony.

Benefits Befitting

The benefits for mentors and protégés are numerous. Knowledge is power, as is passing it on to the next generation. But there are potential problems:

- Mentor trauma created by inappropriate separation
- Hitching your wagon to a star...soon to fall
- Cross-gender mentoring and the gossip it provokes
- Jealousy
- Usurping of ideas by mentor
- Unrealistic expectations
- Investing time/wisdom in an uncommitted protégé

These potential problems can be prevented by being aware and surrounding yourself with a multifaceted network of talented, interesting people. Rather than hitch yourself to a big star, look around your networks for Mentors of the Moment. You get to choose and to refuse according to what feels appropriate to you.

Reminders

➤ Mentors are teachers that help guide our way through the perilous processes of professional life.

➤ Multifaceted networks are full of potential mentors.

➤ There are five types of mentors: peer, informational, retiree, competitive, and godfather/mother.

➤ Protégés can find potential mentors in their workplace, professional organizations, and networks.

➤ A potential mentor can be encouraged to take on the protégé who communicates, pays attention, and listens.

➤ The ideal mentor is the one who is secure, who can "let go" of the protégé and be proud of his/her success.

➤ Mini-mentors or Mentors of the Moment, can contribute to our growth and education and be a resource on an as-needs basis.

➤ The best of mentors are sponsors and supporters who encourage protégés to develop their own styles.

➤ Turnabout is fair play: If you have benefited from having a mentor, you then become one.

12

▷ ▷ ▷ ▷ ▷ ▷ ▷ ▷ ▷ ▷ ▷ ▷ ▷ ▷ ▷ ▷ ▷ ▷ ▷

Just Say No:
to No-Win Networking

The Challenge of Choice

In the 1980s the term "networking" was everywhere. When the professional association's no-host cocktail hour became the no-host networking reception, several colleagues and I shuddered and longed for the days when we would attend a meeting or go to some other function just to chat with people and get to know them. The pressure to network precludes the discovery part of the process of getting to know people that is so important to building long-term relationships based upon rapport and respect.

When we take the time to converse and share ideas, movie reviews, restaurant recommendations, philosophies, values, and laughter, we learn how we can best support the other person's goals and needs. And, even more important, we learn whether or not we want to do so. This does not contradict the concept of "expanding circles" because, in some situations, it is contraindicated.

Unlike family and coworkers, we do get to choose the people with whom we interact (network). That's the beauty of having a network: We create it; we decide who gets to be in it. We get to "just say no" to those whose attitude and/or behavior doesn't feel right. It may just be the wrong fit. We get to trust our instincts about whom we trust.

Gut-level Guide

The voice in our stomachs deserves our full attention and requisite actions. How many times have you "had a feeling, a hunch" about a person you've met at a professional meeting, business exchange, or at the gym and ignored it? Or analyzed it? Or applied logic to instinct, only to find that your initial gut-level reaction was on target and that you should have listened to yourself? (I *cannot* be the only one who has made that mistake.)

Bottom line: People *earn* their place in our networks, whether it's by chemistry or connection or communication that reveals some commonality. It is no one's God-given right, under the guise of the networking process, to be the recipient of our leads, referrals, advice and ideas, and good name.

Maryann Seawall, a writer for the *San Mateo Times,* hit the nail on the head in "Sometimes Networking Needs to Be Short-circuited."[37] She received a call from someone under the pretext of having enjoyed a published interview that Seawall had had with a best-selling author. The caller expected Seawall to ask the author to speak to a group she was starting. When Seawall commented that she knew nothing about the group, the woman was surprised. Didn't she "believe in networking"? Seawall wrote, "Yes and no. I believe in helping others and not being a pest, not imposing and not confusing acquaintances with friends."

In 1991 I attended a professional conference and met a speaker who organized networks and accredited members. The more I listened to him share his views and philosophies on networking, the more uncomfortable I became. He had formalized the process of sharing, all but killing the spontaneity and the joy of it. But I was willing to cut him some slack.

After all, we all have our off days and perhaps he had nervously overstated his case. I was wrong about being wrong—my gut-level reaction was correct. This man handled our communication unprofessionally, which not only wasted my time, energy, and efforts but denigrated them. Yes, we should give and get second chances, as long as we listen to ourselves.

Fact: We get to *choose* our professional and personal associates. Some may protest that this narrows the network. Not really. It only narrows the negative inputs, thereby leaving space for more appropriate members.

On the other side of those who intrude on our time, because they deem us to be in a position to help them, are those people who are in a position to assist, advise, and refer to us. And it still doesn't sit well. The *quid pro quo* tenet of networking requires a return, and the payment of the marker may not be one we want to make. Refusing a favor is an option if the payment doesn't fit. Good advice for the infamous Wall Street highfliers.

Michael Schrage, *Los Angeles Times* contributor, suggests that we "Fire Our Customers!" "Some customers are value-subtracts. What they cost in time, money and morale outstrips the prices they pay."[38] Certain people exact a price that is just too high. We must pay attention to that data, review it, and take action.

While we should make a second attempt to get together with a new contact, we should also listen for the disinterest signals and pay attention rather than pursuing and pestering. What William may have to sell, Joe may not want to buy. Just because we think Al is the best person to give us leads to the manufacturer's representatives, Al may not consider our agenda to be his priority. He may prefer to refer us elsewhere. "I realize you would like me to recommend you to my agent [associate, client], but that is uncomfortable for me."

Yet Another Male-Female Difference

In *Networking, A Great New Way for Women to Get Ahead,* Mary Scott Welch suggests that you "don't have to like the people with whom you network. Men appear to be much less likely to let their personal feelings affect their business dealing...whether this is a front or not, it appears to save energy and keep all bridges open."[39]

Burning bridges is not my suggestion; choosing the bridges you traverse is. In life, those decisions are sometimes made for us. After the October 1989 Bay Area earthquake, the Oakland Bay Bridge was broken, so we traveled the other bridges that connected the Bay Area cities: San Mateo Bridge, Golden Gate Bridge, Richmond-San Rafael Bridge, or Dumbarton Bridge. There are other choices; there always are.

"We should not network with people we don't like or trust, regardless of the deal," suggests Marcie Bannon, conference planner for the National Association of Professional Insurance Agents and inveterate networker. Perhaps this is an area that men ought to model after women, instead of the reverse.

A...MF (Aggravation Management Factor)

Stress and pressure take their toll both physically and emotionally. Stress disability claims are on the increase. Though women are catching up, men still have the dominant market share on heart disease. Maybe interacting with people we dislike is a yet unsubstantiated statistic?

"There is enough required aggravation in a workday, why build it into the network? You have to be willing to take a long-term view versus the short-range immediate benefits of a lead, contact, or piece of information," says Marcie Bannon.

"Greed was fashionable in the eighties; there were shooting stars on the fast track and winning was the watchword.

The nineties focus on reliability; slow and steady wins the race," offers Dan Donovan, vice president of Dean Witter Reynolds.

Exclusion Conclusion

There are legitimate reasons to exclude people from your network:

1. You don't like, trust, respect them.
2. The differences in style are such that you are incompatible.
3. You are unfamiliar with their performance and cannot vouch for it. "Accountability is the one reason I guard my contacts...because I need to know someone before I turn him or her loose on my editors or other valued contacts," explains Gregg Levoy, author and educator, in *This Business of Writing.*[40]
4. You just don't have the time or energy to invest.
5. You realize that you'll be doing all the work...there is no give-and-take.

How to Refuse Entry/Participation

Just because an event is a good networking opportunity does not mean that it is right for you at the time. According to Dr. Geraldine Alpert, Marin County psychologist, we can set boundaries and decline invitations to participate. "While I'm sure I'd enjoy getting together for lunch, my schedule is too tight right now."

Dr. Alpert suggests that we prepare for the second round, in case the person then suggests the alternative of breakfast or dinner. Here's the response Dr. Alpert proposes: "Ordinarily that would be fine but, because of my other obligations, unfortunately I don't have time."

Bored Position: Organization Options

We also get to choose the organizations, officer positions, and boards with which we want to be active. Some people make those choices based on a prescribed, albeit unwritten, code that identifies the path of progress up the ladder. Others of us choose those organizations in which we have a personal or avocational interest. "You retain the option and responsibility to say no to membership in an organization you don't want to join or rejoin. When approached to run for office or sit on a community board, you can say, 'No, thank you,'" offers Lana Teplick, Boston-based CPA.

I once made the mistake of saying yes to an appointed board position in a professional organization. The president assigned me a task that was ominous in that it required skills I did not have (and didn't care to acquire), and utilized none of the skills I did have. The president's mistake was not recognizing those issues and best utilizing my strengths. My mistake was saying yes to be nice because I liked the chap.

Not only was it a nightmare, I also had them! A month later, I gathered all my courage, called my colleague, and quit, with an explanation. That night I slept soundly. Losing sleep over my business or books is one thing; but I cannot afford to do that as a volunteer. If I had only said no in the first place. At that time, I didn't know "no" was an option. Remember, it always is. We get to say no when doing something that isn't appropriate or beneficial to us.

"I am uncomfortable with…"

"That doesn't work for me."

"No, thank you."

These three phrases will serve our professional and personal lives by setting our boundaries and saving our time for what we really want to do and with whom we would like to do it. They will help us move on.

Reminders

➤ We get to choose who enters our network and who does not.

➤ No one is "entitled" to our valued contacts.

➤ We choose the criteria for those with whom we share leads, resources, and time.

➤ We get to listen to the "voice in our stomach." It's our best guide.

➤ We may say "No, thank you" to those who court our connection.

13

▶ ▶ ▶ ▶ ▶ ▶ ▶ ▶ ▶ ▶ ▶ ▶ ▶ ▶ ▶ ▶ ▶ ▶

Moving On, Letting Go, Cleaning Out

Clean Out the Closets of Your Life

Patricia Fripp, internationally acclaimed professional speaker, hired image consultant Diane Parente to help her organize her wardrobe and image. "There were three piles of clothing: one for the poor, one for recycling, and a small pile for me. Some of my favorite items were in the pile for the poor. I begged Parente to let me keep this sweater or that skirt. Parente just shook her head. 'No, these may be favorite items but they detract from who you are now and the image you have chosen.' She wouldn't give in, so most of my wardrobe was given out...to others. I had to learn to let go of that which no longer served me. Cleaning out my closets became a metaphor for how I approach my business and live my life. We must assess, reevaluate, and let go...to make room for the new...be they clients, cronies or clothes. I share that with my audiences as a way of accepting and managing the continual changes in our personal and professional lives."

Eliminate the Negative, Latch onto the Superlative, and Don't Mess with Mr. (Ms.) In-between

When we do clean out our networks, it is analogous to cleaning out our closets. The clothes that Diane Parente allowed Patricia Fripp to keep were the most complimentary, most attractive, and those with the best fit. This I know to be true, as Parente, founder of the Association of Image Consultants, spent five and a half hours with me cleaning out my closet. Because I was happy to use "OPE" (other people's experience) and trusted Diane's judgement, I didn't argue about letting go of my favorite two-piece silk suit. Perhaps I whimpered a bit. Letting go is never easy. There were pangs of regret. I, too, was left with the best and created space for what was to come.

If we do the same "closet cleaning" with our networks and eliminate the negative, we are left with the best—the people with whom we feel great. Why? Once we assess how we feel about each person and with each person, the picture becomes focused. That focus is investing time and energy with people whom we enjoy. With careers, social and family life demanding so much, assessing our networks is the first step in setting our priorities.

The Collectibles

In the process of living and working, it is possible to collect people and organizations. The late Sally Livingston wrote that when she started her business it became difficult to "maintain all of the connections...and add in more of what was needed."[41] She chose: (1) to assess the network that had become unwieldy, (2) to shape it up, and (3) to move on and let go of organizations and people that no longer supported her interest. It is not easy, but it can be done.

Separations are simply difficult and endings are often

nals? Newspapers? Because you canceled the others, you have created time, capital, and space for the new subscriptions.

There are times I have pondered the possibility of cleaning out our networks as grounds for separation or divorce. Could we sue a colleague to whom we gave unreciprocated leads, time, and ideas for "nonsupport"? Or the supervisor whom we could not stand for "irreconcilable differences"? Or the client who dumps us in favor of a younger, more glamorous vendor for "infidelity"?

Fed Up with Feedback! Or, Who Asked Anyway?

One of the ways I clean out my network is to pay strict attention to those who give me unsolicited feedback. Another is to exclude those nosy nuisances who ask personal, private questions that are none of their business. Invasive people are not invited into my network. Do you want them in yours?

Just who are these people telling us how to speak, dress, think, eat, vote, work, etc., when we never asked for their opinion in the first place?

Too strongly worded for those of you who know people who are honest, frank, and/or blunt? They are among those guilty of a curable disease. One of the symptoms of this disease is the uncontrollable need to "share" feedback! Now, we all know people like that, don't we?

Let's get this straight. "Sharing" is what is done with pizzas, sodas, or vacation condos in Maui. It is absolutely impossible for anyone to "share" ideas of how we should raise our children, organize our offices, promote our businesses, stay fit, and, in general, live our lives. What is really being said is what they think—based on their perceptions—which may be myopic and wrong for us. Before we give unsolicited opinions, we should assess our motives. Are we judging, or caring, or understanding?

I think by now you should get the drift. But maybe not. Those of us upon whom have been bestowed *unsolicited,*

excruciating. In my living room hangs a gift, a calligraphic truism:

> *What's let go of provides space for what's to become.*
> —Unknown

Emotional Vampires Suck Energy

There are people in our professional and personal lives who literally drain us of every ounce of energy. Perhaps it may be their less than sunny disposition, constant kvetching,* lack of humor, or maybe they wallow in the Slough of Despond. You already know who these people are: They commute by the "drain train." Every time you come along for the ride, you are exhausted! They are emotional vampires who all but leave fang marks on your neck. They are everywhere: in our offices, professional organizations, and social circles. We may not be able to fire Uncle Bob or Aunt Betty, but perhaps the desire to do so contributes to the high mobility rate of people who move far away from home.

How to Dis-Member

Our networks have organizations and people with whom we should not maintain relationships. "Depending on the length and depth," according to Sally Livingston, "we may offer an explanation that is consistent with our style, time and risk-taking ability."

It's important to know when you have served too long on a board and when to move on so that new people have the opportunity to make a contribution. In some cases, there is no reason to say anything. People do drift apart when common interests no longer exist. Dropping out of an organization may be just as simple as not rejoining. Or an explana-

*See Glossary.

tion to the current president may be more appropriate. How you handle a separation is a case-by-case call.

Quit Dis-Organization

The organizations that supported and served me in my career as an educator have virtually no relevance to my life as a small-business person, speaker, or author.

Go back to your contacts chart that you drafted in chapter 2. Which professional associations no longer apply? Now look at the list of people. Think about them. Fill out this "exorcise":

LIST 1 People With Whom I Spend Time	LIST 2 People Whose Company I Really Enjoy

Is anyone on List 1, but not List 2? Circle their These are the people to be cleaned out of your ne Look again at the lists. Anyone whose name is on List 2, l List 1? Place a rectangle around his/her name. Put thi down, pick up the phone, and call him/her. Schedule a dinner, tennis match or coffee.

Sounds easy, but it is not, because moving on change. Some of those circled names are bosses, cow or relatives who are difficult to dump. Just be less avail you do the above exercise, you will move on and allow for new people and new organizations.

"Drifting apart" is a wonderful term because it ca a natural manner of moving on that ebbs and flows. And are times when changes in our careers and lives cause people to drift back into our lives...in a natural way. V lose temporary touch.

Cleaning Out Your Net

Maintaining a network implies more action than a "d apart." We must make conscious choices, as oppos unconscious ones. Another activity that forces us to cle our network is to go through our card files. Remove fro file the card of anyone about whom you have no recolle Toss it out. If that person recrosses your path in a mem manner, you can always ask for another card.

Go through your card file and remove from it a with whom you have had no contact in eighteen m Place it in the "Not Yet Dead" file that does not h top-priority location on your desk. That creates spac your new contacts.

Cleaning out an information network may be as s as listing the magazines, journals, and papers to which subscribe, circling the ones that are enjoyable and/or he and canceling the subscriptions to those not circled.

What new information would you like? Magazines?

unwanted opinions know that pomposity reflects a very thick skull and no skill.

So let me say it another way. Anyone who is lacking in savvy, or sense, does not belong in my network. There are professional critics and they are hired to review movies, plays, operas, concerts, and restaurants, *not* our lives, careers, choices, or personal tastes. For some, the constant critics are not a problem. To me, they are, and I choose not to allow them in my network.

As a professional speaker, I have chosen a professional speech coach because of her fabulous feedback delivery. Dawne Bernhardt concentrates on the strong points, yet she identifies areas of improvement so nicely that I want to change immediately.

Many of us are subjected to performance appraisals and job evaluations given by people who need a few lessons from Dawne. How we give feedback speaks volumes; why we do so is even more telltale.

I have been told to get rid of my gray hair by people whose advice I never sought. And there are those computer people who are unnerved by my antiquated method of writing by hand—with pencils. More times than I care to remember they have evangelically shared their testimony to the "new, right, fast way." Guess who isn't going to get carpal tunnel syndrome?

We do need feedback and we choose those whose style of advice, ideas, and critiques we can hear. I know I do. And my feedback friends are those whom I trust to have my best interests at heart and who are willing to offer their comments, knowing they are safe to do so. They hear what I say and what I don't say. And not one of them has to ask a lot of questions to get information from me. I am so very comfortable and safe that the information flows. And they never throw a bucket of water to douse my fiery enthusiasm or flaming successes, nor do I do that to them.

Let's Play Twenty Questions: Not!

Whether we are working a room or having a follow-up conversation with a contact, asking too many questions is not a good idea. It is an information-gathering device for the questioner. Such an interrogation always makes me wonder if the data is being gathered for some unsavory reason.

Another view is that a person who asks too many questions rarely avoids the personal ones in the process. I don't want anyone who could be so inappropriate in my network. The person who asks too many questions doesn't convey interest, merely curiosity. They are doing a needs assessment for their sales pitch. Also, they probably are not contributing to an exchange of conversation, ideas, or philosophies upon which rapport is built.

You know your limits. Identify them, honor them, and choose other people who do just that. Be selective.

Leopards and Their Spots: The Derm-Abrasive Dilemma

It is our responsibility to set boundaries for what is acceptable behavior to us. It is further our responsibility to convey those boundaries. Some people may be genuinely unaware of our boundaries because our society has become so lax—or relaxed—about propriety. All we have to do with genuinely well meaning people is to clarify our boundaries, and they will respond with respect for our wishes.

But then there are those who, once informed, transgress again. The choice is up to you. Consider this: Would you trust such a person with a referral to a job, contract or crony? If people ignore your wishes and boundaries, behaving improperly toward you, do you think they will magically transform into considerate, attentive, respectful people?

Leopards don't change their spots. They only lose their abrasiveness by emotional derm-abrasion, or having a spot-lift.

The Wince Factor: Once Is Enough

Anyone who has made you wince—once—is a candidate for learning about your boundaries, which have been transgressed if you winced.

One of my colleagues recently gained weight when he was already very overweight. After we had lunch, a mutual friend asked if I had told him I was concerned about his weight problem. Yes, I am concerned. Did I tell him? Not a chance! You see, he knows he is overweight, he has a mirror and a scale. I didn't want him to wince because I was out of line.

Al Walker, keynote speaker and sales trainer extraordinaire, confirmed my position: "I am a big boy, and on more than one occasion people have felt compelled to point that out to me, as they were concerned about my health. You know, not one of my *real* friends ever said that to me." Another formerly overweight friend of mine quipped, "What they are saying is 'We don't like how you look!'"

I, too, have to restrain myself from an uncontrollable urge to tell my friends how to raise their offspring, yet I have none! How dare I venture forth a suggestion?! At best, I can only give my friends my support and understand that they are concerned.

There are some who espouse the cleansing effect of forgiving and forgetting. Every time I have done the "F&F," I regretted my decision. Second verse, same as the first, a little bit louder and a little bit worse...each time. "Holding a grudge may be the healthiest response,"[42] as it prevents one from getting walloped again. As a colleague said, "The best thing to do is to forgive yourself and to forget them."

That was what one of my clients, a Ph.D. in science for a major multinational corporation, decided to do. When he was introduced as "Dr. Smith" at a party, a guest asked what kind of doctor he was. When Dr. Smith said that he was a Ph.D., he was told, "Gee, you don't look smart enough to have a Ph.D." Did the person intend to be mean-spirited? Who knows or cares? The questions that matters is: Do you want to voluntarily associate with someone so crass?

Networks are created. We get to decide who we want in them, and to take responsibility for cleaning out, moving on, and letting go of those we don't. The good news: We make room for the new additions, the people with high Mensch* Quotients, who do the right things.

Reminders

➤ Life is change; so, too, our networks change to reflect our lives. Change requires us to clean out, move on, and let go of organizations, people, and behaviors that we can no longer maintain properly (giving our time, energy, and support). It is a harsh reality, but a fact of life.

➤ We must eliminate from our networks people who are negative, make us wince, are self-appointed critics, interrogate us or transgress the boundaries we have delineated, and those who draw our energy.

➤ Sometimes we drift in and out of lives, and we do not rejoin organizations. No words or explanations are required.

➤ Some situations call for formal resignation. People of character know when or how to exit graciously.

*See Glossary.

14

▶ ▶ ▶ ▶ ▶ ▶ ▶ ▶ ▶ ▶ ▶ ▶ ▶ ▶ ▶ ▶ ▶ ▶ ▶ ▶

Paying Dues: How to Raise Your M.Q. (Mensch Quotient)

There is no way to get around paying our dues. Whether it's the monetary fee required to join an organization or the payments of the experiences we survive; we do not get our due unless we pay attention to the "Do's." The people who "do the right things" in a courteous, respectful, and honest manner have a high "M.Q." There is no higher compliment than being called a mensch. They are honorable people of integrity and character. They are good people, the people we want to have around in both our professional and our personal networks, because they always make us feel good, comfortable, and special.

The question: How do we find these people?

The answer: Be one.

That's a paraphrase of the old adage about friendship: "The best way to make a friend is to be one." If we pay attention to the Do's, we'll attract those exemplary people in our workplace, in our associations, and in our lives.

Much of the M.Q. is determined by how we communicate and how we behave.

the small society   by Brickman

How to Raise Our M.Q.

- **Participate:** Attend events, join organizations, be active.
- **Work rooms:** Mingle with good manners, charm, and interest in others.
- **Pay** attention: Be "in the moment" in any conversation or activity.
- **Do** your best, be reliable, always work hard and smart. Competence is key to success. "When you do so, others spread the word," according to Rich Gold, international strategic marketing consultant.
- **"Be** a student of the masters. Learning is a lifelong process," advises Patricia Fripp, my favorite professional speaker (and friend), because she lives her message both professionally and personally.
- **Visit** bookstores. There is much to be gleaned from the books that grace the shelves, even if it is the revelation of current trends. Books are friends and teachers. Being aware of your industry or profession and the business climate is crucial. Bookstore personnel are generally people who love books and the written word, and are pleased to assist.
- **Use** your library card. All we would ever want to know about anything is available in the "house of knowledge," the

local library. "Librarians are fabulous resources and are trained to locate and share information," advises Jean Miller, a former librarian who is a successful salesperson and author.

How lucky for us that we can read! It's Mrs. Kurtz's reminder again: The closest thing to knowing something is to know where to find it. The nineties networking version includes the person to whom one may pass the ball for "the assist."

- **Give** praise and compliments; express appreciation. Bill Johnston confirms that by doing so we contribute to those who have done well for us. One of his clients was stumped as to how to fill out the section of a loan application asking his spouse's place of employment. "As she handles the family assets, which are considerable, I suggested he write 'Personal Financial Manager.' When his wife read the application, she broke into a huge smile." Johnson not only gave her a title but gave her the acknowledgement that her contributions were valid and appreciated. An aside: The volunteer efforts of many unpaid, highly skilled, and experienced people should never be underestimated.

  "Pass on the praise of others," suggests Dr. Duffy Spencer, who likes to "good-mouth" people.

  Corollary: *Accept praise* by saying "Thank you."

- **Shine** the light on others. Or, as the adage goes, give credit where credit is due. Frank Reed, Deputy Chief of Investigations, San Francisco Police Department, expressed great admiration for his boss, former Police Chief William Casey. "Chief Casey was always willing to pick the best people and allow them to make the presentations, which lets them 'shine.' It is human nature that we do our best when public credit is given for our efforts."

  As educators, we learned to enthusiastically acknowledge students' successes in public, and to admonish in private. (My belated apologies to any of my former students in Chicago or San Francisco if I broke either of those rules.)

- **Remember** your roots. If we don't remember where we came from, the people who are there will never forget that we forgot.

The most touching acceptance speech of the 1992 Academy Awards was given by George Lucas as he received the Irving G. Thalberg award for special achievement. Lucas thanked his teachers and recognized their contribution to his growth and success. Lucas recalled the impact of the teacher who took the time to whisper words of encouragement in his ear.

In paying dues, we do give "just due" to those who deserve it.

• **Contribute** to the community, whether it's your professional community or that in which you live. Take an active role and contribute time, energy, ideas, and resources. Be it the ballet, local homeless shelter, baseball boosters, Girl Scouts, literacy project, church or synagogue, or your child's school—be involved!

• **Honor** people's time. Donna Epstein responded to my survey question about timely tips with "Look at your watch." This excellent advice was soundly seconded by others surveyed. Carl LaMell offers the same advice for people attending events. "Don't hog the time of the person you need to meet. Remember, if they are important in the community, other people need to meet them, too. You create a better impression by being timely, excusing yourself, and sending a follow-up letter."

Magnificent minglers and knowledgeable networkers are mindful of other people's needs, time, and obligations, and make it easy for them to attend to them.

When *How to Work a Room* was first published, I had to attend an event in New York hosted by Peter Max. It was a benefit for a New York theater group supported by Joanne Woodward. My task was to observe the mingling and to provide a review for *USA Today*. What an experience! The guests appeared to know each other, but I knew no one and I was nervous. Talk about an event with strangers and a reporter. I observed one woman talk to Joanne Woodward for almost twenty minutes, while the line of people who also wanted to meet her continued to grow. Yes, this woman seized the opportunity, but actually lost points because she was so immersed in her own agenda that she did not honor Miss Woodward's time. Miss Woodward treated her most graciously, but had this person paid attention to body language, she would have politely excused herself after five minutes with Miss Woodward. The rest of the agenda could have been covered in subsequent correspondence.

The lesson: Make timely impressions! In person, on the phone, or on paper.

- **Mind** our manners. Paying dues includes behaving in a manner that is proper. Having table manners is important, but having a manner that is courteous, respectful, and appropriate is even more important. Having manners does not equate having money. There are wealthy people who behave poorly, treating others with indifference and rudeness, and there are others who do not have vast sums of money but whose manner is full of warmth, wit, comfort, and charm.

"Civility costs nothing and buys everything," says Mary Wortley Montagu. This was also a timely lesson taught to Frank Reed by his first mentor, a beat cop, who taught Frank how to walk a beat in a rough neighborhood. "He never put people down, even in an arrest, and taught me that you can never lose by being civil to people. It's a lesson that has served me well."

Good breeding is the basis for building friendships, which are the human relations of the business of networking. "Nothing can constitute good breeding which has not good nature for its foundation" (E. Bulwer-Lytton).

- **Accept** responsibility, raise the M.Q. While circumstances may interfere, the mensch accepts responsibility for errors and mistakes, and makes no excuses. People with high M.Q.'s are heard saying, "My error, thanks for bringing it to my attention."

At a party the host told me that he had forgotten a lunch date with an attorney. "I called and said that I had no excuse. I totally forgot, I was so sorry. The attorney was so obviously surprised at my admission that he rescheduled for Monday." **Apologize** when you've erred.

Just because you're stuck in traffic, Reagerson, there's no reason
to waste my precious time, too!

After my lunch with a new acquaintance, he graciously
told me his forthcoming schedule so that I would be
informed of his obligations, which would impact our subsequent meeting dates. My response, which may have been
flippant, was met by a comment that he was "just making
conversation," but the look on his face told me I had been
thoughtless. I very humbly apologized to him, saying that he
was being gracious in sharing his information and that I had
been flippant. I was very sorry. To this day I am embarrassed
by this incident, but glad that I paid attention to his facial
expression and apologized.

- **Understand** that, for the most part, what goes around
comes around. Sixty percent of the survey respondents

indicated this as a tenet of networking. It may come back from another source, but it comes back.

A person with a high M.Q. treats every person with regard, regardless of position. If you're helpful to people, it comes back. If you are not nice, that comes back, too (not all the time, nor as quickly as some of us would like to see the nay-sayers get theirs).

- **Return** phone calls, and in a timely fashion! Seventy percent of the respondents confirmed the importance of promptly returning calls. Cold calls from the boiler rooms may not require the same treatment, especially in the middle of a family dinner when the preference is still to say, "This is not a good time." Keeping phone logs may help.
- **Allocate** the time required to grow a relationship. Friendships do not happen overnight; they are nurtured. Rapport is established and trust is built over time.

    Mihai Radulescu, East Coast entrepreneur, recalls that friendships in his native Romania were incredibly special. "Because of the lack of public information available to us, we relied heavily on sharing thoughts with friends. We had to know who our friends were and who could be trusted—both on and off the job. Our network of friends was truly treasured."
- **Respect** privacy and personal boundaries. Divulge information ever so slowly. Telling too much too soon is too telling. Personal probing questions are prohibited.
- **Do** one thing a day to connect with a new contact or an old friend. Create a weekly reminder list:

Get Rockin' & Rollin'

Mon. — Call Huey Lewis

Tues. — Write a note to George Michael

Wed. — Send an article to Mariah Carey

Thur.— Fax a cartoon to Luther Vandross

Fri. — Recommend Silver Fox Doobey shampoo to Michael McDonald

Sat. — Choose your day of rest, pray with Hammer

Sun. — Refer a publicist to Madonna

Each item on this daily to-do list begins with an action verb. Taking positive action is how we pay our dues, by doing that which we should do.

- **Report** back on the results of the leads, advice, and information. Too many people neglect to do so, and it is potentially embarrassing to the person who hears about the results of effort thirdhand or offhand.
- **Assess** your needs and ask for help. Many people have trouble asking for help, but prefer to give it. We must balance giving with receiving.
- **Call** ahead if you are referring someone to your contact. This way your contact won't be caught off guard.
- **Embrace** diversity of age, ethnicity, expertise in your network.
- **Work** hard. That's why your company is paying you.

Mrs. Predshawn, if you don't mind—a little more *working*, and a little less *networking*?

- **Arrange** to meet associates at trade shows and industry conferences.
- **Stay** visible, informed, and in touch. Bill Gillis said, "To do this, I use 'keeping in touch' cards and I make it a practice to send a few each month. Through the recent use of these cards, I was able to match an East Coast business ethics group and a West Coast anesthesiologist. The ethics group needed a minority member and my physician friend wanted to be more active in business. The doctor is now on their board."

The cost of paying our dues is ever so small and the benefits are incalculable when compared to the cost of doing the Don'ts.

Reminders

➤ We have to pay our dues in order to earn our stripes in the network.

➤ To raise our M.Q. (Mensch Quotient), we must be persons of honor and character, who are courteous, respectful, and comfortable to be around.

To Do's

➤ Work hard and smart.
➤ Be open to learning; it's a lifelong process.
➤ Visit libraries and bookstores.
➤ Attend industry and community functions.
➤ Praise and support others.
➤ Share the limelight.
➤ Remember your roots.
➤ Honor people's time.
➤ Mind your manners.
➤ Apologize when in error.
➤ Return calls.
➤ Stay in touch.
➤ Invest the time it takes to nurture your network.

15

▶ ▶ ▶ ▶ ▶ ▶ ▶ ▶ ▶ ▶ ▶ ▶ ▶ ▶ ▶ ▶

How Not to Be a Networker: The Don'ts and How to Avoid Being a Sleaze

Susan's Slant

The links that we have to other people are fragile and require lubrication to keep them working. Meeting people, conversing, and establishing relationships is easier for some of us than for others. Because the people I've surveyed and interviewed are people in my network, there is a bias: "Susan's slant" is in favor of the warmth, charm, caring, and manners that the people with whom I connect and associate possess. (Their suggestions are properly credited.)

There are those other types of communicators and networkers whose ideas are not offered. Some are as smooth as silk, others so unsavvy that they are transparent. We have lots of names for them—most of which are *im*proper nouns.

The Don'ts

The Don'ts are a compilation of ideas, tips, and suggestions on how to avoid being a "sleaze," as well as how to identify one. You may have more to add. My suggestions may be remedial, but this chapter would not be germane if there hadn't been transgressions.

If we avoid the Don'ts, we will improve our communication, relationships, and networking know-how.

- **Don't** equate the process of networking to a science; it is an *art*.
- **Don't** misconstrue networking to be a sales plan.
- **Don't** be blinded by goals, only guided by them. You have decided to increase your contacts by meeting twenty new people at a two-hour cocktail hour. Meeting your goal mathematically translates into six-minute conversations. As the conversation begins to flow, you must exit and move on to meet your scientifically predetermined numbers game and goal. It's not about how many people you meet, it's about how you have established a connection and rapport.

  In order to play the numbers game, you have to size up people very quickly. In a *Success* magazine article, "Working a Room for Contacts," a fellow advocated the numbers game, making quick decisions as to people's usefulness, and splitting from the conversation to find the person who is more useful (by title, company, appearance). As my grandmother would have said to something distasteful, "Feh!"* "Ugh!"

  This is not networking; it is judging people with a narrow lens, and totally missing the big picture of the networks we bring to each new contact. We all have met people like that, and few people I know would risk their reputations by giving Mr. or Ms. Sleaze access to a colleague, crony, or friend. I know I won't.

- **Don't** be so quick to make surface judgements about others. At a party hosted by a Big Six accounting firm, I noticed that most of the men were dressed similarly. There were few women attending, but they, too, were conservatively attired. One man wore an alpaca sweater, Perry Como–style, and his

*See Glossary

demeanor was very casual. I shared my observation with Peter Meeks, then a partner, now an assistant dean at UC Berkeley's business school. "Susan, this guy can dress any way he wants; he could buy and sell all of us in this room."

- **Don't** use a name to gain access without the permission of that person (Becky Gordon).
- **Don't** foist your business cards upon people nor deal them out to others before a conversation occurs.
- **Don't** offer unsolicited opinions for the benefit of those who never asked.
- **Don't** talk about the monetary terms of your last deal; most of us know to divide that figure in half and subtract your weight...in ounces.
- **Don't** ask for more than people can give.
- **Don't** take credit for the ideas, concepts, and words of others (it's called plagiarism, violation of copyright or stealing).
- **Don't** blame others for your missed deadlines and unfulfilled promises.
- **Don't** be invasive and ask too many questions.
- **Don't** forget to contribute to conversations.
- **Don't** forget to think before speaking. Pregnant pauses are sweet silences.
- **Don't** ignore signals (body language, gestures, words, tones).
- **Don't** use disparaging humor.
- **Don't** overstay your welcome.
- **Don't** cop a touchy-feely (keep your lips, hands, and arms to yourself). "Friendly" pinches, squeezes, hugs, and kisses may not be considered so by the recipient.
- **Don't** use suggestive language.
- **Don't** be an opportunistic glad-hander. Be in the moment with people.
- **Don't** misrepresent a sales event as a social party (Miss Manners).
- **Don't** pursue, pester or push people; that will lose the link, and the contact. Let it go.
- **Don't** bad-mouth people. One never knows how that can come back to haunt you. A local city supervisor gave his annual holiday party. Upon being introduced to his assistant,

she mentioned her former employment. I smiled and shared the name of my buddy who used to work with her. Her disparaging remark about my friend revealed her lack of political savvy and sense.

- **Don't** send unsolicited résumés to people who don't know you, and don't expect to receive them. Effective communicators apprise people ahead of time.
- **Don't** forget to do your homework to prepare yourself.
- **Don't** deflect compliments; they are gifts. Acknowledge the giver by saying "Thank you" (Donna Epstein).
- **Don't** get discouraged; the process will work if you understand it.
- **Don't** forget to say "I'm sorry" when you have erred, as well as "I don't know," "Please," and "Thank you."
- **Don't** lead people on; tell the truth.
- **Don't** compromise ethics for a quick buck (Chris Bigelow).
- **Don't** be afraid to try something new; you can always return to the old way (Chris Bigelow).
- **Don't** be afraid to be afraid (Doug Sharpe).
- **Don't** drop a colleague, client or customer *because his/her timing is different* from yours. This month's turndown could be next year's mega-contract.
- **Don't** discriminate against people; be discriminating among them.
- **Don't** complicate the concept of expanding and overlapping circles of contact with petty power plays.
- **Don't** forget that cross-gender networking is impacted by the differences in conversational styles of men and women.
- **Don't** be one of the "hail-well-met and hardy" boys!

Reminders

➤ Don't forget to pay attention to paying dues and raising your M.Q.

16

▶ ▶ ▶ ▶ ▶ ▶ ▶ ▶ ▶ ▶ ▶ ▶ ▶ ▶ ▶ ▶

Group Gusto: New and Old Ways to Network

A disclaimer is in order here. This chapter provides a method for locating, identifying, and starting groups or networks à la Mrs. Kurtz (my fifth-grade teacher): "The closest thing to knowing something is to know where and how to find it." If you really want to enhance your personal and professional life by being part of a network, this chapter provides brainstorming support.

The Three Formats

There are three types of groups and formats that offer a network of people:

1. Formal Network Groups

The primary purpose of formal groups is the exchange of leads. These groups may also exchange support, resources, advice, and ideas; but leads, contacts, and tips are the top priority.

2. Semiformal Networks

Semiformal groups are formally organized, but the major purpose is not the networking. It may be educational, informational or regulatory. These groups are available for you to join, if you decide you want to do so.

There are also clubs and groups that are private and exclusive. If joining one of them is of interest, your network can assist you. They exist in every city, and a membership in such a club may serve you (even if they won't serve me). Caution: If the exclusivity is exclusionary, and if you have political aspirations, you might want to reconsider membership.

There are as many groups as there are special interests and job descriptions. In the directory for the American Society of Association Executives, you will find a membership of over 20,000 national, state, and local trade and professional associations. These organizations provide a host of services and benefits for their members, not the least of which is a network of people who share that interest. There is a preexisting commonality, a basis for conversation with any member.

3. Informal Groups

Informal groups are the ones you hear about that are not affiliated, have no charter, and, perhaps, no dues. They may be a Friday night poker club, or a menopause support group, or a Monday morning bridge and breakfast group.

Groups at a Glance

Once you have assessed your network of affiliations, you see the gaping holes. You can join a preexisting group or, if there is none for the purpose, you get to start one.

The first thing to do is to get a pad of paper and jot down all the different groups that are in your life. Check the "Take Stock Exchange" chart in chapter 2. Either write on this page or on your paper pad.

	Formal Network Groups	Semiformal Networks	Informal Groups
P E R S O N A L			
P R O F E S S I O N A L			

Is every aspect of your life and your interests represented by each group supporting it?

List those areas for which you would like to have a group for resources, input or support:

1.
2.
3.
4.
5.

Determine if there is a local or national organization that matches your needs. You can find out by:

1. Looking for it in:
   - Yellow or white pages of the local and special phone directories
   - Business and special events calendars of local papers
   - Chamber of Commerce newsletters and directories
   - Libraries: public, company, community college, etc.

2. Asking:
   - Friends
   - Neighbors
   - Classmates
   - Colleagues
   - Coworkers
   - Associates
   - Butchers
   - Bakers
   - Candlestick makers

Don't forget: The people we know have vast networks of people we don't know but to whom they may provide a link.

A Start-up . . . for Company

"If no group exists that you would like to join, start one," advised Sally Livingston, my femtor. In the early eighties, she saw there wasn't an informal setting where entrepreneurial women could meet, chat, and brainstorm. She started the Poker Club, a Friday morning breakfast gathering of consultants and others gainfully self-employed. The time and place were set, but there was no formal agenda, nor were there speakers. The participants were the focus.

Sally's words echoed in my ear as I realized that my business groups were all women; the male professional perspective was missing for me in the mid-eighties. So I started a monthly No Name Network, which lasted for a year. The fun part was that I invited the people I knew, respected, and liked, and they invited others they knew, respected, and liked. It was a casual yet very supportive group of terrific, hardworking professionals. We brainstormed, assisted, commiserated, and applauded each other. We laughed and we listened.

Cerebral Salons for the Smart

A recent phenomenon was featured in *Newsweek*: the rise of salons, not for hair, but for hair-raising conversation.[43] The idea isn't a new one—the Algonquin Roundtable is a famous salon of yesteryear. People do want to converse, discuss, exchange, expand, and evaluate ideas and information. Book clubs have provided this environment for discussion with a focus on literature. Paula Kahn, advertising executive, was in one such club when she lived in San Francisco. "The camaraderie and conversation were definitely the part I looked forward to each month."

John Naisbitt predicted the trend toward "high touch" because of the presence of high tech (*Megatrends*). The salons are a manifestation. To me, that is wonderful news; the art of conversation is not dead.

Many of the groups that exist are focused on "doing"; we are moving in the direction of groups focused on conversation and communication. The contribution of words and thoughts is one that nurtures the network and, as people relate to one another, solidifies.

This is good news for those of us who are not interested in bonding on the bike path. Cerebral connections are "heady"!

Starting a group requires thought, organization, time, and effort. If the informal group or network you start meets a need or interest, then the return on investment will be worthwhile.

A Network Quilt

Maybe you share an interest in sports, theater, road racing or quilting. Becky Gordon, quilter for seventeen years, has quilted with a local group of women. They contributed to the Names Project quilt and have a nationwide group of people who share their craft, interest, and talents. It's a fine craft with a long history, and the people who do it become part of Becky's network. When in the course of conversation Becky learns someone quilts, there is an instant connection of common threads.

Onetime Lead Leads to Lifelong Friendship

The result of my investment in starting the No Name Network was meeting a friend's friend with whom I shared an instant connection. It was sparked by our Chicago roots and developed into a cherished friendship. Linda Mantel and I have supported each other through both pleasurable and painful experiences in our professional and personal lives...through thick and thin.

If these informal groups are so wonderful, maybe we can franchise them! In a way, we do that. Many originally informal groups are the bases of formal organizations and associations. While we can formalize groups, we cannot formalize the process of developing friendships.

Still, I asked franchise development consultant Sandra Lipkowitz about the possibility. "While it is an interesting thought, franchising friendships is not possible. We can join

12-3

Why don't we start an old boy network club and
then sell franchises?

Reprinted by permission:
Tribune Media Services

groups, attend events, introduce people to each other with great enthusiasm, which predisposes people to like each other. In essence, we are *sharing* our networks of contacts, cronies, and friends. But friendships are not chocolate chip cookies. In franchising, we duplicate, but every friendship is unique. Susan, it is a half-baked idea!" I knew that, but, as it has been said before... it couldn't hurt to ask!

A relationship that blossoms into a true friendship is the most precious of diamonds: There is great clarity, many facets, and it's true to color. The shapes may vary, but the value only increases with time.

Formal Club—Forming Friendships

The Dover Club in Houston, which started as a networking club, "has gone beyond just business support and become a community of entrepreneurial support," according to Sandy and Donna Vilas in their book *Power Networking*. "We believe that if you give more than you expect to receive, you'll get more than you ever expected."[44]

Irv Spivak, of IME Telecom Corp., helped establish a business lead exchange group through the San Francisco Chamber of Commerce. Five years later there are five groups of over 150 people, which, according to Irv, "has spawned disciples throughout the Bay Area." The groups have dues, a noncompetitive clause, and a tardy policy. Irv explained, "Would you want to do business or refer business to a person who has already demonstrated a punctuality problem?" Good point! "Having a formal business networking group allows us to train others to think of us. The results: There are twenty-nine salespeople listening for our needs, and formal leads groups lead to building relationships in business."

Groups: a Partial List

Formal Leads Groups:
- Business network groups
- Professional and trade associations
- Company clubs and groups (some larger companies have their own Toastmaster chapters)
- Civic and community groups
- Informal groups

Formal Networking Clubs:
- Leads Club
- Le Tip International
- Business Alliance
- National Association of Female Executives

Professional/Trade Associations:
- Check local Chamber of Commerce directory
- Yellow Pages
- American Society of Association Executives directory
- Local Societies of Association Executives

Service Clubs:
- Soroptomists
- Rotary
- Lions
- Kiwanis
- Friends of the Library
- Toastmasters
- Shriners
- Democratic Clubs
- Republican Clubs
- Ballet Boosters

Charity Organizations

Religious Groups (church, synagogue, temple)

Health, Crafts, and Sports Clubs

There are thousands of organizations, networks, and groups. Decide what works for you. The groups you choose may assist you in career aspirations, but whatever you decide to join, remember that building a base of business referrals is based on establishing rapport, trust, and respect. Once those three ingredients are present, contacts grow into relationships that enhance our personal and professional lives.

As with every group that has gathered since biblical times, a codification of the laws, values, and rules provides order and standards of behavior.

Reminders

➤ There are several types of groups one may join:
- Formal lead exchange clubs
- Semiformal professional and trade associations
- Special interest groups
- Informal groups

➤ Assess what groups you would like to join.

➤ There are 20,000 associations and groups where people gather to exchange ideas and information, to gain updated education, and to lobby their cause to the government.

➤ There are private and public sector, profit and nonprofit, civic, service, charity, religious, and sports organizations.

➤ Some groups are heterogeneous, others are homogeneous.

➤ We can locate the existing groups through our networks and the local Chamber of Commerce.

➤ Let your fingers do the walking—use the Yellow Pages.

➤ If no groups exist, start one.

17

> ▷ ▷ ▷ ▷ ▷ ▷ ▷ ▷ ▷ ▷ ▷ ▷ ▷ ▷ ▷ ▷ ▷

The Gospel According to RoAne... Revisited

THE TEN COMMANDMENTS
of
Communicating and Connecting:
The "Newer" Testament

We create the network of sources and support that comprise our personal and professional safety net. To be able to do this, we must connect with the people we meet, be considerate of our contacts, and communicate with our words and our ethical behaviors. The following commandments provide a Ten-Point Plan that will contribute to a viable and valuable network of colleagues, cronies, and friends.

I. THOU SHALT BE A MENSCH.
Treat people with respect, courtesy, integrity, truth, and honor.

II. THOU SHALT FOLLOW UP AND FOLLOW THROUGH.
Do that which thou sayest thou shall do...and report back in a timely manner.

III. THOU SHALT PAY ATTENTION TO OTHERS.
By listening with one's ears, eyes, head, and heart.

IV. THOU SHALT NURTURE THY NETWORK.
Touch base with calls, cards, clippings, and faxes when thou needest nothing from thy contact.

V. THOU SHALT TREAT PEOPLE AS PEOPLE.
Treat them not as contacts made for thy professional purpose.

VI. THOU SHALT "GOOD-MOUTH" PEOPLE.
Praise people and pass on the praise of others!

VII. THOU SHALT ACKNOWLEDGE ALL SUSTENANCE WITH THY PEN AND TABLET.
Thank those who have gifted thee with time, food, ideas, support, leads, laughter, and love.

VIII. THOU SHALT PERFORM GOOD DEEDS.
Ye shall **reciprocate** those deeds done on thy behalf.

IX. THOU SHALT TEACH THESE COMMANDMENTS DILIGENTLY TO THY STAFF, STUDENTS, COLLEAGUES, CRONIES, AND CHILDREN...**By Thy Example.**

X. THOU SHALT HAVE FUN AND BE OF GOOD HUMOR.

▶ ▶ ▶ ▶ ▶ ▶ ▶ ▶ ▶ ▶ ▶ ▶ ▶ ▶ ▶ ▶ ▶ ▶ ▶

For Those Desperately Seeking Susan

Susan RoAne is a widely recognized keynote speaker who gives programs for corporations, organizations, and associations. Susan's presentations are known for their practical information, humor, and results.

For further information about her informative and entertaining programs, please contact:

Susan RoAne
THE ROANE GROUP
14 Wilder Street, Suite 100
San Francisco, CA 94131

(415) 239-2224

▶ ▶ ▶ ▶ ▶ ▶ ▶ ▶ ▶ ▶ ▶ ▶ ▶ ▶ ▶ ▶ ▶ ▶

Glossary

The following are some Yiddish terms I've used in the book, plus others that you may use and find useful and/or amusing. Although these are terms I know, I acknowledge Leo Rosten's *The Joys of Yiddish* as my reference.

A-ha! An expletive of illumination. (I was surprised to see this in Rosten's book as a Yiddish expression. For two decades I thought it had its roots in the California Human Potential Movement!)
"A-ha! That's why the board held their meeting in private."

Chutzpah *Classic usage:* Gall, brazen nerve. *RoAne's usage:* Courage, gutsiness. "It takes chutzpah to initiate conversations."
"The crook embezzles from the company and then requests a farewell party! That's chutzpah!"

Fe! or Feh! An exclamatory expression of disgust and distaste.
"This sleaze undercut me on the bid and then asks me to dinner . . . Feh!"
"They are serving pasta with scallops and kumquats? Feh!"

Kvetch To fuss, gripe, complain. The person who does that.
"Mark is constantly kvetching about his boss."

Maven An expert, knowledgeable person.
"With the new portable phones, the manners mavens have their work cut out for them."

Mazel Tov! Good luck, congratulations.
"I am so pleased that you were promoted. Mazel Tov!"

Megillah Anything long, complicated, boring.
"Tell me the results of the negotiations; I don't want to hear the whole megillah."

Mensch An honorable person of integrity; someone of noble character with a sense of sweetness as well as what is right and responsible. To call someone a mensch reflects deep respect.
"Dan Donovan, my stockbroker, is a real mensch!"

Mensch Quotient or M.Q. A numerical assessment of a person's character based on his or her treatment of others based on a scale of 1 to 100. (Thanks to David Schultz for sharing this concept with me.)
"She called me to say she would be fifteen minutes late for our meeting. Her M.Q. is increasing."

Nosh To eat in between meals. A snack, a small portion, a nibble.
"I prefer to nosh all day than to eat three meals."

Nudge To pester, nag; to give a surreptitious reminder of a job to be done. The person who is a nag.
"He kept on nudging her to stop smoking."

Oy vay! A lament, a protest or a cry of delight. It expresses anguish, joy, pain, revulsion, regret, relief.
"Oy vay! It is such a tragedy to lose a home in a fire. Thank heaven the family is safe."

Schlemiel A consistently unlucky person; a hard-luck type; a social misfit.

"Robert is good-natured, but can't seem to do anything right—he's such a schlemiel."

Schlepp To drag, pull or lag behind. Someone who looks bedraggled and schleppish.

"Don't schlepp all those packages, you'll hurt your back."

Schmooze Friendly and gossipy prolonged conversation; act of chatting *with* someone.

"Harry and Stan schmoozed for an hour at the party."
Incorrect: "Harry schmoozed Stan at the party."

Shpritz To spray. The liquid that is sprayed.

"I shpritzed myself with too many different perfumes."

Shtick A studied, contrived piece of "business" employed by an actor (or anyone); a trick; a devious trick.

"Watch him use the same shtick on this new client."

Tchotchke A toy; a trinket.

"I refuse to buy my clients tchotchkes with my logo on them."

Yenta *Classic definition:* A gossipy woman who does not keep a secret. It may also refer to a man who does the same.

Newer usage: Since *Fiddler on the Roof,* a matchmaker.

"Be careful of what you say, Rhonda is a real yenta." (Classic)

Endnotes

1. Marilyn Ferguson, *The Aquarian Conspiracy* (Los Angeles: J. Tarcher, 1980), p. 35.
2. Susan RoAne, "Networking: Beyond the Buzzword," *Meeting Manager* (New York: Meeting Planners International, Oct. 1985), pp. 8–10.
3. *Webster's Unabridged Encyclopedia Dictionary* (New York: Random House, 1983).
4. Judith Briles, *The Confidence Factor* (New York: Master Media, 1990), p. 199.
5. Tom Stanley, "The Secret of Millionaires," *Success* (New York: Lang Communications, 1985).
6. Michael Korda, "Do These Things Before Forty," *Success* (New York: Lang Communications, 1985).
7. Robert Kriegel and Louis Patler, *If It Ain't Broke, Break It!* (New York: Warner, 1991), p. 159.
8. Bruce Feld and Christine Evatt, *Givers and Takers* (New York: Macmillan Collier, 1983).
9. Susan RoAne, loc. cit.
10. John Naisbitt, *Megatrends* (New York: Warner, 1982), p. 22.
11. Mollyanne Maremaa, phone interview, Mar. 10, 1992.

12. Harvey Mackay, *The Harvey Mackay Rolodex™ Network Builder* (Secaucus, New Jersey: Rolodex™ Corporation, 1990), p. 20.
13. Ibid., p. 21.
14. *USA Today,* "Reader Poll," Feb. 9, 1990.
15. James Challenger, "Stay Visible No Matter Where You Work," *Executive Female* (Nov/Dec. 1991), p. 9.
16. Paul Stern, *Straight to the Top* (New York: Warner, 1990), pp. 106–8.
17. Ibid., pp. 110–11.
18. David Lewis, *The Secret Language of Success* (New York: Carroll & Graf, 1990), p. 225.
19. Marilyn Moats Kennedy, *Office Politics: Seizing Power, Wielding Clout* (Chicago: Follet, 1980), p. 16.
20. Stern, Ibid., p. 22.
21. Max De Pree, *Leadership Is an Art* (New York: Dell, 1989), p. 11.
22. Miss Manners, Tribune Syndicate, *San Francisco Chronicle*.
23. George Walther, *Phone Power* (New York: Berkely Books, 1987), pp. 89–90.
24. Miss Manners, syndicated column, *Chicago Tribune*.
25. Ellen Goodman, "Telephone Tag of the '90s: Not Talking to a Person, a Time-saving Technique, Is the Goal," *San Francisco Chronicle,* Jan. 7, 1992.
26. Miss Manners, "Call Waiting Calls for Consideration," *San Francisco Chronicle,* 1991.
27. John Flinn, "Voice Mail: Not the Answer," *San Francisco Examiner,* 1992.
28. Ibid.
29. Debby Love-Sudduth, phone interview, Feb. 1992.
30. "Money Beat," *Marin Independent Journal,* 1992.
31. Korda, "Do These Things," p. 112.
32. John Sculley, speech, Feb. 25, 1992.
33. Kennedy, pp. 146, 149–50, 154–55.
34. Michael Korda, "The Strength to Shut Up," *Self* (July 1984), p. 48.
35. Susan RoAne, "The Art of Being Mentored," *San Francisco Examiner,* 1983.

36. Korda, "Strength to Shut Up," p. 49.
37. Maryann Seawall, "Sometimes Networking Needs to Be Short-circuited," *Peninsula Times-Tribune,* Mar. 21, 1984.
38. Michael Schrage, "Fire Our Customers!" *The Wall Street Journal,* Mar. 15, 1992.
39. Mary Scott Welch, *Networking, A Great New Way for Women to Get Ahead* (New York: Harcourt Brace Jovanovich, 1980), pp. 76–77.
40. Gregg Levoy, *This Business of Writing* (Cincinnati: Writers Digest Books, 1992), pp. 120–21.
41. Sally Livingston, "Careers Series," *San Francisco Examiner,* 1982.
42. George Gatze, excerpt from interview in *Glamour, San Francisco Chronicle,* 1987.
43. "Talk About My Generation," *Newsweek* (Mar. 23, 1992), pp. 66–67.
44. Sandy and Donna Vilas, *Power Networking* (Houston: Duke Publishing, 1991), p. 118.

▶▶▶▶▶▶▶▶▶▶▶▶▶▶▶▶▶

Additional Resources

Susan RoAne. *How to Work a Room.* New York: Shapolsky, 1988.

Susan RoAne. "Paying Up Pays Off." *San Francisco Examiner* Careers Series, 1982.

Susan RoAne. "The Grapevine Is a Goldmine." *San Francisco Examiner* Careers Series, 1983.

Susan RoAne. "How to Avoid a Splitting Headache." *Meeting Manager.* Dallas: Meeting Planners International, Aug. 1988.

Susan RoAne. "Dealing with Office Politics." *San Francisco Examiner* Careers Series, Nov. 28, 1983.

Susan RoAne. "Fed Up with Feedback, or Who Asked You Anyway?" *Meeting Manager.* Dallas: Meeting Planners International, July 1987.

Susan RoAne. "Reaching for a Career Mentor." *San Jose Mercury-News.*

Index